On The Right Side Of The Road

Tom West

McGilligan Publishing

3707 Cypress Creek Pkwy Ste 310 #505

Houston, TX 77068

On The Right Side Of The Road

Tom West

McGilligan Publishing

3707 Cypress Creek Pkwy Ste 310 #505

Houston, TX 77068

WWW.MCGILLIGANPUBLISHING.COM

Copyright © 2025

ISBN

Hardcover: 978-1-965560-89-1

Paperback: 978-1-965560-92-1

Printed in the United States of America

Second Edition

Contents

Introduction

Perhaps you are wondering what it is like to drive the big rigs for a living. Wanting to share my experience with anyone interested in this career, I decided to write stories about this particular subject. They come right from my personal experience and travels while driving trucks. For the most part, they are true. I also have thrown in a few other things which have happened to me in my seventy-five years of life. I have been told my life has not been, by any stretch of the imagination, a normal one.

I have driven a truck because it is one thing thanks to my father, I learned to do very well. I think I may have diesel fuel flowing through my veins, and it has always been something I could do to restore my self-confidence.

Many of the stories are from a diary I kept while driving for a company in Arkansas and one in New Mexico in the late 1980s and early 1990s. I have changed a few of the names to protect the innocent as well as the guilty. I have no desire to become prey to an unscrupulous attorney who might fall into the employ of someone, or someplace, that I might have offended with this writing.

My career in trucking started when I was sixteen years old. I went to our local bank in the Texas Panhandle, and my dad went with me to co-sign, I think. I walked out of there with a loan to purchase a 1956 Ford grain truck.

But trucking was not my only calling in life. I have been in the farming business oil business for nine years, and owned and operated an insurance company. I was a vice president in banking for eight and one-half years and a salesman for dealerships selling Mercedes Benz, Jaguar, and Honda. And still managed to drive the big trucks from time to time.

With my ego leaving me at about the same rate of speed as my hair was turning gray, this transition was not as difficult as it might seem to one who would think that being a vice president in banking would not allow anyone to go back to being a trucker. I have found the social esteem associated with a vice presidency will get you a cup of coffee in a restaurant if you also have in your possession about a dollar you are willing to part with.

I left the farming business in 1968 and drove a cattle truck and a grocery truck for about two years. I then worked for a large natural gas company in New Mexico for nine years. I moved back to Texas at my wife's insistence and drove a cattle truck for six months. I took over a closed insurance agency and operated that for about a year when a banker friend of mine asked me to go to work for him in his bank. I told another bank president friend of mine about this offering. He asked me if I was interested in banking, to which I replied, "I have not given it much thought." I became a banker in the second man's bank a month later. That falls into the category of "he made me an offer I couldn't refuse." I stayed in banking for eight and one-half years, then went back to driving a truck again for my mental health and physical well-being.

I believe there were only two kinds of bankers in the 1980s: the crook, which nothing bothered, and the honest banker. The honest banker, to lower his Maalox consumption, is now doing something else, even driving a truck. Some bankers have managed to remain fairly honest and, for the sake of "never say quit," are still in the banking business. Most of the ones I knew are now in the vault, counting quarters and humming to themselves The Battle Hymn of the Republic or Amazing Grace.

One Monday morning in 1980, I walked into the bank lounge for a cup of coffee. There were about fifteen women of the bank's employ also having a cup of this wonderful black pick me up. The rather outspoken receptionist said, "I heard something about you over the weekend that I don't believe." As she was saying this, she was looking me over from head to foot. "What was this unbelievable thing you heard, for I might be able to shed some light as to whether it is true or false," I responded. "I heard you once drove a cattle truck, and I can't imagine you with cow manure all over you," she said. I think this is because I usually was one of the best-dressed male officers in the bank. "Well," I said, "I have driven a cattle truck, and I have had cow manure all over me. But there is also a second verse to that song. I could change clothes, put on my boots and jeans, and do it again tomorrow." Little did I know that is exactly what I would do, except for the manure. One does not get that messy hauling ice cream in a truck unless you are parked next to a couple of J. B. Hunt trucks.

I did all of these things with just a high school diploma and a Ph.D. from the school of hard knocks. I also hold a graduate degree in shaky investments and hasty decisions.

Boy, how things in the trucking business have changed. My dad drove a truck in the 1930s. Hauling cotton from southwest Oklahoma to Houston. The trucks of that day were Chevys with six-cylinder engines, burning gasoline. They would run about forty miles per hour. Dad said he made eight dollars per trip. There were no sleepers on these trucks either.

Today, the drivers can make eighty thousand per year, and everything is computerized. The company knows where you are all the time. No log books because the logs are on the truck's computer, so no cheating.

Some of this story was written thirty years ago. This is written as it happened, but as I am Southern, some of the facts could have gotten bigger in the rendition. This is not all bad because, in the south, bigger is often better.

It is not my intention to offend anyone or any trucking company in this writing. This is my point of view which may or may not be in the mainstream of thinking throughout the industry. There are certain parts of the country I would not choose to inhabit simply because I have no particular liking for them. I am reporting the facts as I saw them, similar to the way the news media does in its reporting of the facts in a news story. Sometimes, I may lean to the left, sometimes to the right, but I think, at least in this country, it is better to drive on the right side of the road.

Dedication

This book is dedicated to my father, Arlie West, for vaccinating me with a phonograph needle and transfusing me with Gypsy blood. My dad was, to me, and always will be, one of the greatest men in the world. He taught me the many values that I have held on to all my life. My dad had a unique way of doing things and was a hard man to work with, but we never had to question his love for us. My father was a man who loved all little children, for he believed they were God's precious gifts to us. He is one of the only men I know who had respect from all who have made his acquaintance. If charity is a good virtue to possess, then it can be said of my dad he was a good man.

I would also like to thank my best friend in life, my wife Diana, for her unwavering devotion and love. Without her inspiration, I would not have the guts to write this or anything for fear of failure. She always tells me I have never failed, but I have always worn a parachute with my hand on the ripcord.

Chapter One

While living in Wisconsin, I left the banking business over a dispute with a senior vice president. Enough was enough in the banking industry, and I promptly got a job selling Mercedes Benz automobiles. If you are selling Chevys, you sell cars. If you sell Mercedes Benz, you are selling automobiles. This is what the General Manager of the Mercedes Benz dealership told me. He had been selling Buicks at a dealership owned by the same man who owned the Mercedes Benz agency. He always dressed a little better than the rest of the salesmen, and I was told this is why he got the job as General Manager in the Mercedes Benz dealership.

You are probably wondering what this has to do with driving a truck. Well, I am getting to that part by telling you HOW I got from banking to truck driving again, so be patient and read on.

You also might be wondering what dressing nicer than the rest of the salesmen in a Buick store has to do with becoming the General Manager in a Mercedes Benz dealership. I have often wondered that myself and the only people who might know the answer are the ones who have worked in the car-selling game for more than five years.

However, I have made this observation: the qualifications for management in a car dealership has no relationship to management ability. It is not unlike many other types of businesses I encountered during my tenure as a banker. The brother-in-law system is used for management qualifications in many areas, but it is running rampant in the car business.

1

This General Manager said many profound things during the five months I worked there. When I started, this speaker of wisdom told me I probably would not sell a car for the first month because they were very high-priced cars. I would need time to develop the expertise it would take to sell to the type of individual who drove Mercedes Benz, he explained. The third day I worked there I sold a used Mercedes Benz that had been on the lot for over a year. I sold the car for the price posted on the window, not knowing that five thousand dollars had been reduced on the price of it because of the length of time it had been on the lot. I was also naive enough to think this would make the manager happy. You see, the manager also sold cars along with his duties as boss. I found out later if a salesman could outsell him he was instantly on this man's hit list. I found this to be true after being there for five months. One morning, the manager said something very profound to me just after I had come into work. "You are fired for reading the newspaper in your office," he said. Reflecting on the incident, it must have happened because I had read all the goody out of the paper before he had time to read it.

I had already decided it was time to get out of that part of the country and get back to a place where my Texas accent was better understood. Milwaukee is no place to live when you enunciate words like I do: "Heil low" is not a proper greeting to the typical Milwaukeean. Nor is, "Howdy, how y'all doing."

I make my way to Albuquerque, New Mexico, after a short stay in Tucson, Arizona, with another mismanaged Mercedes Benz dealership. In my sixth month there I sold more cars than all the rest of the sales force put together. The following month, as a reward for my efforts, I was demoted to the used car department for fear of offending the older salesmen who worked there. I stayed long enough at this dealership to find that in the used car department, my income went down by two-thirds. I promptly decided to bid them farewell and move to Albuquerque.

But before I said adios, I waited until after I attended the on-track driving program for Mercedes Benz held at Willow Springs racetrack in Lancaster, California.

Those four days were to be the highlight of my automobile-selling career. I have always been fascinated with driving, and going fast was not totally left out of my curriculum. I spent some time in the mid seventy's racing motorcycles. I have also done some drag racing. I always wanted to drive a road course and do it right. Here was my opportunity to do both. Not only were we instructed by some of the best professionals in the business, but we were also driving the very finest cars in the world as a bonus. There wasn't a Datsun in sight. We drove Mercedes, BMW, Jaguar, Acura, and even a domestic tank.

If you have ever been around people who work for the high-dollar European car companies, you will know why I said domestic tank. They are more prejudiced than a southern republican politician with Civil War ancestors. The week after the trip to the racetrack, I quit the Mercedes dealership and moved to Albuquerque, New Mexico.

It was the beginning of the summer of 1989.

For the past six months, I have been selling Hondas at a local dealership in Albuquerque. I was offered a job at another car dealership as the finance manager. Now, this was what I thought would be the type of work I should be doing because of my background in banking. How wrong I was or was about to learn how wrong this way of thinking would be. After only two weeks in this position, I found out why some automobile dealerships have gotten the reputation of being, well, you know what I mean, a little less than honest. The management was stealing about four to five hundred dollars per contract. When I

3

discovered this fact and brought it to their attention, I was asked to leave.

I was at the end of my career in the automobile business, and my spirits were as low as a snake's belly. What was I going to do? Now, I have never been without an idea, so I bought fifteen hundred dollars' worth of welding equipment and started making sculptures out of horseshoe nails. I did this as a hobby fifteen years ago and figured that this could be a way not to be interfered with while working. I would make these little Western sculptures in my garage and would have no one to answer to but myself.

It worked like a charm. I even won second place at the first art show I entered. Wow, I thought I was going to be a famous artist and financially independent within a short time. I only encountered one small problem. The little sculptures did not sell for very much. In fact, they hardly sold at all. I barely made enough money to pay the expenses for the trip to the art show. Now, at my age, I was not willing to become a starving artist and live out of the McDumpster until such time as fame and fortune would arrive. I could see it was fourth and ten, and it was time to punt.

After talking it over with my wife, she agreed that maybe driving a truck would help clear my mind and bolster my confidence. I had visions of adventure out on the road and coming home for a day or two every week. Little did she or I realize that, in reality, this vision wouldn't be true.

So, I called a couple of large trucking companies and was told I needed two years of recent, over-the-road driving experience before they would hire me. I read an ad in the local paper the next Sunday advertising for drivers by a local trucking company. On Monday, I called them and was told the same thing as the ones before. I asked the safety director if they gave a road test to anyone they might look at to hire, and he said they did. I said, "Why not give me a road test? You will know if I can drive one of the things or not." He agreed and set a time for me to take the road test.

They unhooked the tachometer on the truck I was to drive to make the test even more difficult. After we got back to the truck terminal the man who gave me the test went to the safety director. He told him they could send me anywhere in the United States they wanted to, and that very afternoon, I became a truck driver again.

It seems as though whenever I get overly frustrated with doing whatever I am doing at the time; I can always turn to the driving skills I learned early in life.

Well, after about a year of driving for them, I became disgruntled with this company. I took a load to California for them with a firm understanding that I needed to be home in a week. The reason for this request was because we were moving into a new place and I needed to be there to help with the move. After numerous assurances that they would get me back to Albuquerque as I asked, I took the load. Low and behold, they kept me running around the West Coast for 2 weeks. Every call to the dispatcher, I was told the same thing...this will be the last run, and we'll get you home. When I finally got back, the move was done and I was a very unhappy camper.

Needless to say, I quit and contacted a trucking company I had heard about in Little Rock, Arkansas, that was supposed to be a good one. After talking to them over the phone, I decided it was time to take a trip to Little Rock to check them out further. My wife, Diana, had a couple of days off so we drove from Albuquerque to Little Rock to do just that.

The next morning, I found myself sitting in their office finding out about what they hauled and where, what they paid, and checked out their equipment. I also met the dispatcher who was there and visited with him for a while. They were anxious

5

to have a driver closer to the West Coast, so it seemed like this would be a good fit. While there, I did all the paperwork needed and all the other things to sign on with a trucking company to drive their equipment.

Since I lived in Albuquerque, we decided I could hitch a ride from one of their trucks that was coming back to Little Rock from the West Coast. I would ride with him to their office to pick up my truck and get my first load assignment.

Back home, I packed my duffel bag with clothes and toiletries, my CB Radio, and, of course, my briefcase. The briefcase was used to store my logbooks, lots of note paper, note pads, pens, pencils, my truckers' road atlas, and my two friends, Smith & Wesson, along with extra cartridges. A small sleeping bag was also included with a blanket and pillow rolled inside. The rest of my stuff, including a lot more clothes, I could pick up from the house when I was heading to the West Coast. And, of course, the small 10-inch TV that I usually had in my truck, which provided entertainment when spending a night at a truck stop.

Most of the news going on in the country and the world was from the stations on the truck's radio or other truckers via my CB Radio. This was in the day of no cell phones so the CB was your friend and source of communication with other humanoids while driving down the road. Truckers would talk for many miles on them. Some of the conversations were very interesting, to say the least. This was also known as entertainment in some cases. And was helpful with road conditions, directions, places to eat, and where the super troopers might be lurking to snag a Big Truck for speeding.

The call came from the home office about the trucker leaving the West Coast and when he would arrive at the truck stop near my house. Close to the appointed time of arrival, I loaded my stuff into the pickup and my wife drove me to catch my ride to Little Rock.

A few days later, I found myself sitting in their office, waiting for a truck.

Chapter Two

Monday, March 25th. I went to the office at about 8:00 a.m. There, Jerry, the dispatcher, wanted me to drive his little brother's truck because he wanted off for a few days. The truck is an almost new red Freightliner with a 42-inch sleeper. This is a very plain Jane truck in looks and appointments.

It is hard for me to look at these two guys and tell that they are brothers. They do not look anything alike. Jerry is short and chubby, while Gary is around 6' 3" and slender. They may have had different fathers together, for I was told they are from Kentucky.

We get into the truck at 1:00 pm and head east on I-40 on the way to Sikeston, Missouri. At West Memphis, we turn north on I-55. We go about fifty miles and come to a construction area that has a posted speed of 45 miles per hour. I am sitting in the right-hand seat, and we are swapping lies about everything. We are going about 65 miles per hour when we top the overpass in the construction area. Just on the other side of the overpass is an Arkansas Highway Patrol car lurking in the median, waiting for the high-speed large car (trucking term for Big Truck). This highway patrolman, I observe, has the "I got you on the radar" grin on his face as we are passing by.

Gary gets a ticket for doing 59 in the 45-mph construction zone. He was fast on the brakes but not fast enough. The ticket will cost him $67.25. He tells me his wife will kill him when he gets home. Only if she is 6'4" and weighs 225, I think to myself.

This is one of the costs of doing business as a driver in the trucking industry. You have been gone from home for three weeks and get a ticket for speeding trying to get to the house to see the little woman. Or a large woman, depending on your taste, or what might taste good to her.

We get to his house in eastern Kentucky at 10:00 pm after loading the ice cream in Sikeston. It takes him and his wife thirty minutes to unload his stuff from the truck. Oh, by the way, his wife is not six feet four inches or 225 lbs. She is about 5' 4" and 120 pounds, and the only way he should fear for his life is if she comes out of the house with a shotgun. With all the kissing and hugging, either he didn't tell her about the ticket, or she was just very glad to see him. He hands her his clothes and his personal items from the cab of the truck for half an hour. It has filled the back of a half-ton pickup bed. I didn't know you could get that much into the cab of a truck and still leave room to drive.

I install my own CB radio, put my clothes away, get all my personal things straightened out, and start driving toward Atlanta, Georgia.

At about 2:30 in the morning, I am just south of Nashville, Tennessee. I am tired and very sleepy and need to make a pit stop. I started asking myself why in the hell am I doing this again. What am I doing this far from home, in the middle of Tennessee, and fighting sleep? I must be crazy. Now, I am about seventy-five miles from Atlanta, and I am still talking to myself to stay awake. I am tired, hungry, sleepy, and mad at myself for just being here.

I finally get to Atlanta, Georgia, and it is very big, much larger than I expected. I find the street I am looking for after about a half-hour of going back and forth and all around. The warehouse district is about twenty miles from the downtown area and is about the size of Amarillo, Texas. I find United Refrigeration which has approximately one hundred fifty loading docks. My appointed place to unload is at door number seventy-seven, the ice cream area. I get unloaded about 8 a.m. after the warehouseman wakes me twice to tell me something. These guys in the ice cream areas are really nice, in fact too nice. They will come out to your truck to tell you just about anything that could have waited until later. Now I can't go back to sleep and go call my dispatcher on the phone. They tell me I will reload with ice cream in the same door in about two hours. I finally do get some sleep, and they get the truck loaded with ice cream at 2:30 pm on Tuesday, March 26th.

There are three fellows in this area. One has a beard that hangs halfway to his pants. I asked him why the long beard, and he told me it was for warmth. I guess one would need something like that to work in a room that is below-freezing all the time. He is a very friendly guy and reminds me of what one of Santa's little helpers would look like.

I get my load papers, and I go around Atlanta on I-285 South until I come to a TA (Truck Stops of America) truck stop. I fuel up, eat, and take a shower. I get back into my truck, drive all the way to Hickory, North Carolina, and get there at 1:00 a.m. Wednesday, March 27th, I crawl into the sleeper, and I sleep like a baby until 6:30 in the morning. Now I feel a little better after eating breakfast and finding the place I am to unload the ice cream.

Murphy's Law strikes again. I have gotten, in my state of tiredness, the unloading order backward. I have never done this type of thing before, and I am embarrassed to myself. I am at the last stop, about 150 miles away from where I should be unloading. After calling my dispatcher to advise him what has happened, I haul ass, and ice cream, to Columbia, South Carolina, with great haste and with the gusto of a hound dog. The company I worked for didn't have governors on their trucks, so there were no engine restrictions on speed to hamper me from getting to the proper place as fast as my angel could fly.

I get the ice cream off at 1:00 in the afternoon, and then I go as fast as I can to Darlington, South Carolina. I am only an hour and fifteen minutes late for this stop. They don't say anything. They are a small distributor, and I think they are glad to get their Mickey Mouse Bars.

The remaining frozen treats I can't unload until tomorrow so I head north to Marshville, North Carolina, where an old friend of mine has lived for the last ten years. We have been buddies since high school. The road winds through the countryside, and when I finally get to Marshville, I stop at the Dairy Queen. I walk over to a payphone and call Jim. I tell him, "You are always wanting me to come to see you." He asks," When can you come, and where are you? For some reason, I don't think you're in New Mexico."

I tell him, "I'm at the Dairy Queen in Marshville." He says, "You are not; yes, you are. How else would you know we have a Dairy Queen.? It's just opened!"

He comes to get me and takes me to his house. They are very surprised to see me and want to know why I am driving a truck, among other things. While the hamburgers were being cooked on the grill, I gave them the what fors and whys of me driving and for a different company. Being in this part of the country was only temporary; I told them until I started regular runs to the West Coast. And, of course, I told them how the company in Albuquerque really got me upset when they ran me around the West Coast when they knew I needed to be home in a week. After cussin' and discussin' the ways of big companies, we enjoy a pleasant repast–that is, a meal, then visit and swap lies until about 10:00 in the evening.

Jimmy and Patty Stumpf are in the cattle business, registered beef masters. He is another person who has had a change in life like mine. Jimmy is a former executive in the fund-raising business. One of his former employers, a very

11

famous actor, whose name is associated with this charity, found out he was sidelining in the cattle business. His boss told him to either get out of the cattle business or else. Jim's reply was, or else what? They told him being associated with this charity and his cows were not compatible. To this, his reply was, "I quit." He moved to Charlotte and went into the cattle business full-time. Jim told me something terrible that evening. He is also raising Sheep. I told him that no self-respecting Texas Cowboy would be in the Sheep business.

He promptly said, "This is not Texas; it is North Carolina, and the Sheep are making me more money per acre than the cows. I am not in this business for my health." I then asked, "Does your family know?"

I knew a cattleman in Texas in the early 1960s who just about disowned his youngest son for buying a lamb for a 4-H project. Then that darned kid went and named the critter "Chore-do." Every time his father asked him if he wanted to keep that damn sheep, his reply was, "Chore-do."

After leaving Jim's place, I get into Charlotte, NC, about 11:30 pm, fuel up, and take a shower before going on to Hickory to unload in the morning. I get to Hickory at 1:00 a.m. and go to bed at Hungry Homers.

Thursday morning, I get up and go into the truck stop for breakfast. There are only four or five tables with people eating in the whole café. There are also four waitresses, and it takes ten minutes before one comes by and wants to know if I have ordered. I say, "Not in this lifetime, I haven't."

"Well, what will you have?" she asked. "I don't think I will have enough time available to eat breakfast because I unload in about three hours from now. So just bring me a cup of coffee, please," I answered. If I had ordered breakfast, I might still be there waiting for it.

At five minutes until 8:00 a.m. I arrive at the parking lot of MDC. I have an 8:30 appointment to unload. Now they tell me the real appointment time to unload is 1:30 pm. The trucking company's unloading time and the real unloading time can vary by a vast margin. You see, the dispatcher, knowing that Murphy works out here, will tell the driver he has an early delivery time because if he said it was early afternoon, the driver would not leave the truck stop until noon, and then his truck might not start, or worse.

When I get into the building where the unloading takes place, one of the receivers starts telling me about a Navajo Truck Lines driver who got mad when he was told it would cost him $100 for a lumper. A lumper is a hired hand who does the unloading of the truck. The lumper doesn't work for the warehouse but is recommended by them if the driver doesn't unload it himself. The cost of the lumper is usually paid by the trucking company delivering the load.

After a heated discussion, this driver promptly gets in his truck and drives off. While still in the heat of rage, he calls his dispatcher, and the dispatcher tells him, "You will unload the truck yourself; we won't pay $100. We will pay you thirty dollars to do the unloading." Well, to make a long story short, the guy brings the truck back and unloads it. I think the conversation went something like this: "We told you that you would need to unload the truck yourself because we can't pay that amount." This sounds nice, but the part of the conversation I left out was the part about being fired if you drive off the lot. Driver not so smart after all.

Thursday evening, I am now at the same truck stop I was at last night. I called my dispatcher, and he told me the normal load I would have picked up has now been canceled out for this week. I think to myself, maybe it's because this is Easter week, and tomorrow is Good Friday. The dispatcher tells me to call him in the morning.

Well, who should I meet in the truck after playing a game of pool? The Navajo driver of unloading fame. I stand and watch the game for a few minutes. Then the Navajo driver starts telling me about this morning's fun over unloading his truck.

Oh, I think it appropriate to mention at this time this guy looks just like "Chuck Baby" and talks just like him, too. Chuck Baby is a truck driver from the plains with a verbal reputation that spans far and wide.

He tells me how he really gave them hell over the unloading of his truck this morning. He doesn't know I have already heard this story from the warehouseman at MDC. The driver's rendition of the events is totally different from the one the warehouseman had told me earlier.

To hear his side of the story, the warehousemen are akin to the "Gestapo," and he told them a thing or two before he totally cowed down and unloaded the truck all by himself.

The more he talks, the bigger his stories get. I look down and notice that the entire floor is covered with bovine residue. This stuff will stain my socks if I stand here and listen much longer. An old and wise trucker told me, "Always wear cowboy boots in the truck stops." To hear him talk, not another truck driver in the whole world is as smart or makes as much money as he does.

He now tells me he also ranks among the best pool players in the country and could make as much money shooting pool as he drives a truck. The kid, who is his current victim, leaves after this game. The Navajo driver asked me if I would like to play. I am reluctant to be victimized by a pool shark such as him, but I consent. After a thorough trouncing in three games of billiards, the Navajo driver, who was trounced, suggests we go into the café and have a cup of coffee.

His stories got less and less potent during the course of the pool games.

The waitress pours the coffee. He tells me the way I play pool I should come back to his hometown. He also tells me I could earn a good living, especially the way I play the game. I might be better than the average pool player, but I am not in the "Minnesota Fats" category. One amazing thing about this driver is he was from Indiana. Only a truck driver from Texas could have told bigger lies than this guy did.

I have often wondered why some people look at me and think I have "Easy Listening" tattooed on my forehead. I guess they are so full of crap that they just want to share, and I truly believe I should have some of that wonderful stuff for myself. They also might think because I am from Texas, they can spread their bull crap to cover up my own personal brand of the odious substance.

φ

In 1982 I was a Vice President in a bank in Oklahoma. One of my customers, who owned a printing company, made me some cards. These cards were the same size as a regular business card, only they read, "My Card Sir. I am from Texas and somewhat of a bullshitter, but occasionally I like to listen to a professional, Please Continue." I never had one of these cards with me when I needed one.

It is now 9:00 p.m. Eastern Standard Time, and I have been filled so full of the before-mentioned substance that I take a laxative and go to bed. Tomorrow morning should be very interesting, to say the least. If I don't rid myself of this collected residue, I might go blind or worse.

Friday morning, March 29th. I can see...even though I know I have lost at least ten pounds.

15

It is raining at Hungry Homer's truck stop. I have called my dispatcher three times now, and they still don't know about the load they said I would have today. This load is supposed to be going to the West Coast and right past my house. Yippee…

It is now 11:00 a.m., and I have just been informed that instead of a load of floor covering headed to the West Coast, I am to go back to Atlanta, Georgia.

There I am to pick up another load of ice cream which is to load at 5:00 this evening. It is raining even harder now. If I am going to get to Atlanta by five in the rain, I will need to go nonstop and in a hurry.

Today is Good Friday, and as I turn south on the interstate highway, I realize before I go a mile the entire state of New York and half of Jersey is out here. I get about twelve miles from Charlotte, and traffic is slowing to a crawl. A wreck, a one-car rollover. One car is in the ditch, but the rubberneckers have halted forward progress. At this rate, I might get to Atlanta by noon tomorrow. Going through Charlotte is a mess. Heavy traffic, heavy rain, and the inevitable construction zones. The radio is saying there is a good possibility of severe weather. I wish the disk jockey was out here with me. He would see severe as more than just a threat. New York drivers and rain are a combination that is like driving through a Texas Tornado. My radio is now saying there are tornadoes reported around Greenville, South Carolina. This is going to be a fun day in the trucking business.

I get to Atlanta at 4:30 p.m., and as Minnie Pearl would say, "I am mighty proud to be here." I really made good time, with the weather and the traffic being so heavy.

They get the ice cream loaded very quickly, and I head to the TA truck stop on I-285 to spend the night.

I am scheduled to unload some of the ice cream in the morning here in Atlanta. Jerry tells me the owner of the place where I am to unload was irate after the last delivery, and they want everything to go just right. Maybe I should deliver the Mickey Mouse Bars and Disney Pops on a silver pallet or something. This is the trucking business, and he shouldn't expect things to go right.

I arrive at the truck stop, have dinner, and call my wife, Diana. A driver sitting at the next table to mine starts talking to me. By the time we finish the conversation, two hours have passed. He is from Dothan, Alabama. He tells me he has a degree in business from a university in Alabama. He said he hated working inside so much that he started his own business and that it had recently failed. He is now driving a truck and likes it very much. His next trip is to Salt Lake City. After he hears that I am from Albuquerque, New Mexico, he asks me what kind of country he will see on this trip. He says he has never been west of the Mississippi River. I tell him about the prairies, the mountains, and the hostile Indians he is likely to encounter crossing this wild and untamed part of the country. I wonder how much of that crap he will believe. I wonder if his wife will let him go. I tell him I am kidding about the hostiles, except on a Saturday night.

"You aren't going through there on a Saturday, are you," I asked.

In the meantime, the waitress stopped by at least six times to ask if I wanted anything else. I tell her no, not unless my iced tea glass becomes empty. I wonder what size tip she will expect for six return visits. I should have told her I was homeless and that this was a good place to stay for a while. This would be to lessen the shock from the size of the tip.

I take a shower and go to bed. I am up at 6:00 a.m. and go into the café for coffee after finding where I'm to unload

17

from a map that is on the wall in the truck stop. It is in downtown Atlanta. Why would anyone want to have an ice cream distribution warehouse in downtown Atlanta? While I drink my coffee, I have wild visions of weaving in and out of all the traffic going into the downtown area.

Not to worry, it is Saturday. I unload five pallets of ice cream at Tasty Ice Cream at 8:00 a.m., and the irate owner is as nice as anyone could be. In fact, he is downright pleasant. It makes me wonder what the truck driver was like who made the last delivery there.

The rest of the ice cream does not unload until Monday morning at 11:00 a.m. in Hickory, North Carolina. I can take my time going back to Charlotte, even a little nap at a roadside park along the way. I stop at an Arby's Roast Beef for a sandwich, then go on to the TA truck stop in Spartanburg, SC. It's nap time again. This could become likable except for the money. The fact is that in this business a driver doesn't make much money going one hundred miles in two days. Miles equals money on your paycheck because drivers are paid by the miles they have driven. So much for a fat check on this run.

I decided since I had the weekend to go two hundred miles, I would call my old friend Jim and see if they were doing anything this weekend. I don't expect them to be taking their daughter on an Easter egg hunt. She is a junior in college and is twenty-one this year. If not, we could play some golf. I call, and Patty, Jim's wife, tells me to come on. They will put some steaks on the grill, and Jim would love to play golf. She tells me Jim had said to her that morning he wished we could have had more time together.

"Perfect," I tell her, "I am headed your way." I look at the map, Road Atlas to see the easiest way through Charlotte, for they live on the east edge of town. I pick a highway that looks like it goes around Charlotte to the south. Wrong. It goes through downtown with 5,000 stoplights that I manage to find all red. I finally get to his house and park the truck next to his barn. Remember, he is in the cattle business, and ranchers have barns. It is close enough to the house, so I can keep an eye on the "reefer" and the ice cream. Trailers hauling frozen goods or refrigerated stuff have refrigeration units on them to control the interior temperature as needed or required. Wouldn't want the Mickey Mouse Bars to melt before some little kid has the opportunity to freeze his teeth trying to bite off one of Mickey's ears.

Their grilled steaks are delicious and worth the wait. The price is less than at the truck stops. Little did I know the money I would spend the next day at the golf course would buy many steak dinners. You are probably thinking Jim took me to the cleaners on the golf course. Wrong.

After a good night's sleep in a real bed and a good shower in a house bathroom, I was ready for the day. So, Jim and I head for Pinehurst, North Carolina, to play a course known as the "Pit." It is a beautiful golf course, with a mighty handsome price for its use, as I was about to find out. At this point, I should bring to your attention the fact not all truck drivers would be thrilled to have a weekend off and want to play golf at the "Pit." But remember, I once was a banker, and bankers play golf as sort of a religion. Some are tennis players, but other professions have weak people in them, too.

I once played tennis back in 1978, and while trying to hit a high and short lob through the body of my opponent (ex-wife), I broke my left leg and actually hyperextended my knee from the sheer force of the swing. The editor of the local newspaper just happened to be playing in the next court. Now, old Hawkeye was the kind of reporter who knew a good story when he saw one. I think he was there gathering material to write a new soap opera. Well, he came running over to where my broken body was lying in state because two EMTs were fiddling with a stuck zipper on the leg splint. He turned his tennis racket around to where the handle was pointed at my face and asked, "Would you like to make a comment to the press about the game of tennis?" My comments were printed, with proper editing, on the front page of the local rag in the next issue. I have been unable to handle the abuse of even driving by a tennis court since then. I think all of the local tennis players must have taken lessons from John McEnroe.

Back to our golf outing. The guy behind the counter tells me the price of the greens fee, cart, and rental clubs. I know how the driver who got the speeding ticket must have felt when he said his wife was going to kill him as I reached for my Master Card. At $90.00, this ain't cow pasture pool. This is championship golf here. We play twenty-seven holes, and the next morning, I am stiff and sore, and my wallet is smarting, but we both shall heal in time.

Believe me when I say, "This is better than six weeks in a cast after playing tennis."

Monday morning, Jim and I go into town for breakfast before I head to Hickory to unload the rest of the ice cream. These folks here in Marshville are some of the friendliest folks I have ever encountered.

While we are eating, three or four different people stop by and talk to us for a while. I have noticed in these parts the conversations usually ranged from race cars to fishing. The Winston Cup type of racing, with "What do you think of Darrell Waltrip or Dale Earnhardt?" The fishing talk is the same here as it is in Oklahoma or Texas. Every place I have been in this part of the country, except for the frozen food lockers, has items for sale from stock car racing.

I arrive at the warehouse in Hickory for my appointment to unload at 11:00 a.m. But these warehousemen must have partied hard over the weekend because they are taking a break every fifteen minutes. They start on my truck at 1:00 in the afternoon, and it is going to make me late for the last stop, which is at 3:00 p.m. With all their cigarette breaks, I now can't make the 3 p.m. appointment in Charlotte.

I made a call to my dispatcher, and I got it rescheduled to unload at 8:00 a.m. the next day. I head for Hungry Homer's truck stop again. I have been here so many times in the last seven days I think when I walk in, I should say, "Hi- honey, I'm home."

Tuesday, April 2nd. I have unloaded the remaining ice cream in Charlotte and have parked the truck at a 7/11 store not far from the food warehouse that received Mickey's frozen delights. I called my dispatcher, and he told me the floor covering load was back on again. I go back on the "call me back in an hour" routine again. The load of floor covering is going to Los Angeles, California and I would be going by the house. I would like to see my wife before she forgets what I look like.

At 4:00 p.m., the dispatcher is giving me the details of the load. I am to go back to Atlanta and pick up more ice cream for Orlando, Florida. I look on my map and can't find a route that goes anywhere near Albuquerque, New Mexico, where I live, and where my wife was the last time I saw her. I ask the dispatcher, "What about the floor covering to Los Angeles?" The answer is not intelligent enough to repeat, so I guess I will go to Atlanta for more Mickey Mouse Bars.

While I was on the phone with the dispatcher, I told him that at the last stop, the Warehouseman turned down one box of ice cream bars. He tells me he doesn't know if they will charge me for it, but I can do anything I want to with the stuff. Eat it all, he says. Not wanting to ruin my schoolgirl figure I think I will pass on that idea. I am walking back to my truck when a guy asks if he could buy the box of ice cream bars and what kind they are. I tell him they are Mickey Mouse Bars and I will

21

take twenty dollars for them. I have never seen a guy get a twenty out of his wallet so fast. I wonder if I sold them too cheap. I guess I will find out when I get my settlement sheet from the company. If part of the load is not accepted, the driver is sometimes charged for it. When a warehouse rejects something, it stays on the trailer, and the driver becomes the proud owner of whatever it is. Crazy since the driver didn't load the stuff in the first place. Oh well, that's how it is.

Chapter Three

Wednesday, April 3rd, I am loading more of these frozen goodies, that will wind up at a 7/11 store next to Disney World in Orlando.

I head out for the swamps of Florida and realize I am running out of clothes, more specifically, droopy drawers, underwear, to be exact. I stop at a 76 truck stop on I-75, and I commit a cardinal sin. I am a Hanes man myself, and they only have Fruit of the Looms in colors. My bottom is destined to be covered in as many flavors as the Mickey Mouse Bars come in. My wife will be surprised if I ever get home to show them to her. After a shower, I stand in front of the mirror to admire the newly purchased, colored undies. "Now isn't that special." Red Fruit of the Looms. With these on, I won't be able to keep my wife's hands off me.

Nothing wrong with that. I wonder why my cowboy upbringing prevented me from wearing colored undies earlier in life. Hell, I feel like the country hick who came to town for the first time and found nearly everybody wore shoes. Now that I am showered, shaved, and admired, I shall get my Fruit of the Looms on down the road to Florida.

Thursday morning, April 4th. I am sitting in an Orlando truck stop on the "call me back in an hour" program again. The Mickey Mouse bars have been delivered, and I need another load to make tracks, hopefully to the West Coast.

I have been told I would not like Florida. It would not be appropriate for me to tell who said that to me, for it might cause the people of Florida not to like this person who doesn't like 300 percent humidity mixed with sand and saltwater, snakes, and alligators. One saving grace is this person does like orange juice. If all the people in Florida are like the ones I met at the place where I unloaded in Orlando, I, without further investigation, would agree that Florida is a place not to be liked. These people did not know much about what they were trying to do.

The dispatcher sends me to Super Foods to get a load of, you guessed it, ice cream for Atlanta. I check the map, and behold, that isn't even close to the West Coast. Maybe tomorrow?

Now at Super Foods and after checking in at the office, I head to the breakroom. Some of the forklift drivers were there, and I couldn't help but listen to their conversation. I don't believe a group of sailors of old could be that foul-mouthed. If these guys at Super Foods made love as often as their language indicated, they would not weigh one hundred pounds collectively. In this humidity, they would probably disappear altogether.

One of these guys tells me their new supervisor was fired from UPS and that is why he was hired at Super Foods. That makes sense, doesn't it?

This supervisor walked around the pallets of ice cream for over an hour. I have no idea what he was looking for. Then he walks to within thirty or forty feet of the break room and makes a hand gesture that I should go to where he is standing. This type of hand gesture alludes to a suppressed attitude problem. I hate to leave the warmth of the break room for the thirty-two degrees of the warehouse. I asked what he wanted, and this supervisor told me I would need to restack some of the pallets, for they were stacked too short. I should point out that the only time restacking is necessary is when the product is stacked too high. I tell him I need to be back in Atlanta at 8:00 in the morning, and he has screwed around for two hours doing a twenty-minute job. If he wants this stuff restacked, I told him he should take off his heavy coat and get to work because I am going to Atlanta right now. I also told him this load was put on the pallets as ordered by his company.

With great authority in my voice, I say, "You just sign the damn bills, and I will get out of here." He signs, and I leave before he realizes that a dock supervisor's calling in life is to do anything possible to make the truck driver miserable. As I drive through the gate, I am thinking to myself, *"What a dummy, no wonder they fired him at UPS."*

The load is safely delivered in Atlanta at the appointed time, and once again, I am headed to Orlando to deliver more Mickey Mouse frozen delights. Are you surprised? The company should call me the King of Ice Cream, and my truck and trailer are the Ice Cream Express.

Finally unloaded again, I go to a nearby truck stop for the rest of the night and get some sleep. I get up at six in the morning, go into the café for some breakfast, and call my dispatcher again.

There is a man in the truck stop that has a knife sharpening booth. I strike up a conversation that starts something like this, "How are you doing this morning?" In the next one- and one-half hours, I not only find out the answer to my question, but I also have never heard so much from so few in my entire life. It must be the easy-listening sign on my forehead showing up again.

His name is Clint Brown, from Abilene, Texas. I think I have finally met someone who has done it all. He even gave me a couple of pictures of when he was a country and western singing star. These were the type of pictures that stars usually hand out. He has on a hat with a special force's pin on it, along with a few others that I don't recognize either. I wasn't in the service. I should point out at this time that Clint is handicapped somewhat from the injuries he suffered in the war. His left arm just hangs there and doesn't move on its own power. His left leg will move, but he is very crippled. His handicap is purely physical; it has not slowed his talking down one little bit. He is not sitting on his purple heart and crying about why people don't care about Vietnam veterans.

With his handicap as bad as it is, I think it would be easy to just give up. As in the country song by Hank Williams, I don't think Clint did it that way. I don't think "give up" is in Clint's vocabulary. He is still out there in a truck stop working every day sharpening knives and bending ears. If I sound like I am being critical, I can assure you I am not.

I am not sure I believed all I was told by Clint Brown. But I am sure I admire him very much for his just keeping on. I also would like for him to call me a friend because I will always consider him one of mine.

It is 10:00 a.m. and overcast here in Orlando, with the humidity at least 300 percent. I think I know how the wicked witch in The Wizard of Oz must have felt when she was doused with water. I don't know if I would melt, but I believe wilting is a very real possibility today.

I live in Albuquerque, America, where the humidity is so low that when it does rain, the drops only have a fifty percent moisture content. The reason I refer to the place as Albuquerque, America, is that outside of the southwest, many people who are unschooled in geography think Albuquerque, New Mexico, is part of the country which is located just south of the United States. I have even been asked for my green card a couple of times back east. I am amazed when people confuse my Texas drawl with a Spanish accent. The more of this country I travel, the more things amaze me.

New Mexico is like some foreign countries in that it has a King—Governor Bruce King, to be exact. He is an Anglo, with a partial Spanish accent, and south of the border ways. One day, while crossing the Texas Panhandle, just before the New Mexico state line, I heard a driver say on his CB, in New Mexico it is believed that "se habla Español" means "hell yes, I work for the state."

Well, it's calling time again, and I want to hear about a load to the West Coast so I can go by the house on the way there. "It's" Calling Time Again" would make a good title for a country song. Clint Brown could write and sing it and revive his singing career. Until I started driving a truck again, I didn't listen to much country music. I have always liked music, even country and western, but I have not been an avid listener in recent years. Until I got back into a truck, I might have thought Garth Brooks was a social disorder associated with fishing polluted mountain streams.

It's 11:15 a.m., and I call back again. This time, Bill Dawson, the owner of B&R Transport and part-time dispatcher, gets on the phone with me. He says there are a couple of loads going to California, but he gave them to other trucks that are currently in this same area. He didn't tell me why, just that "they" were in the same area, and I thought, "So *am I*."

Bill is about five feet and seven inches tall and wears Western clothes. He has a full-length picture of his wife on his desk. In the picture, she is a very trim woman. He should cherish this picture of his wife because when I saw her, she had increased in stature and in girth considerably. If size were a consideration in who is really running this trucking company, Bill's wife is chairman of the board.

Finally, he gave the reason for no load for me to the West Coast—because loads out of California are going to be slow for the next couple of weeks, and he doesn't want me to be stuck out there. How thoughtful of old Bill. He must really like me and hate the drivers of his other trucks he has just sent with loads to the West Coast. I am honored and getting more homesick by the minute. I feel much taller after the way my leg has just been pulled. I also think I am starting to smell another week out here hauling ice cream. I may have a desire to try covert action against Baskin-Robins if I ever get home.

At this point, I think I should explain why I want to go to the house. I know a person who drives an over-the-road truck is going to be away from home for a while. When I left my home for Little Rock, I had been told that I would take a truck back to the West Coast. Upon my arrival in Little Rock, I was told that the truck I was supposed to get had been delayed in New Jersey. I sat in the Holiday Inn for five days waiting for it. That is when the brilliant plan was hatched for me to take the dispatcher's brother's truck and haul all this ice cream in the southeast. When I left my house, I thought I would only be gone for a few days. My clothing supply has run out, as I have already mentioned in this writing. Naked truck drivers would probably not be allowed by state statute or my modesty. Besides, I believe I would get a terrible rash from the vinyl seat.

It is now 3:30 p.m., and I have been given a load of produce from Florida going to Little Rock, Arkansas. I had a long conversation with Clint while waiting for the load. He has told me about his five wives and many other things too numerous to mention. I have been having daydreams about flying from Orlando to Albuquerque all afternoon. It is amazing what a person can think of when he is sitting just waiting for something to happen.

When I was a kid and got sick, my mother would take me to the doctor. The worst part of the experience was sitting in the lobby waiting to be called in by the nurse. One could imagine all sorts of things the doctor would find wrong. Would I ever get out of the place alive or with all my body parts intact?

Enough of this dreaming, I am going to the wonderful town of Belle Glade, Florida. I found it on the map, and it is on the southern shore of Lake Okeechobee. I head south on Highway 27, and the traffic is very heavy. Once I get to the southwestern edge of the lake, the traffic thins out along with most other forms of civilization. The only buildings I have seen in the last twenty miles are ones with signs out front saying "Alligator Farm."

It is starting to rain, and as I drive through a little town called South Shore, I don't see one sign that says Belle Glade. It must be further east on this highway where I will turn north on Highway 80 to Belle Glade. I get about five miles east when two trucks pass me. I ask on the CB where Highway 80 turns off. They reply, at the last stoplight in South Shore. Oh no, I hate it when that happens. There are not many places to turn a truck of sixty-five feet in length around here.

On the map, this place is covered with small horizontal lines which mean "Swamp." For an Old Texas kid, "Swamp" means cootie-infested water that you sink in. I see a small area at the side of the road where there has been a little extra asphalt added to the shoulder. I get as close to the right side as I dare and turn with all it's got. I am headed back to South Shore and I tell the guys on the CB that I have made it. One of the drivers tells me I must be a lucky S.O.B. because if I had gotten off the road, I would have been in the swamp up to my ass. This would also have caused a rash, but I have made the U-turn, and I am going in the right direction. Now, to find that signal I missed in the rain, the dark, and the poor placement of highway signs. I find it and head on down the highway to Belle Glade.

Once in Belle Glade, I stopped at a service station and asked for directions to the Towel Distributing Company. He tells me how to find the place, and I find a building saying Towel Distributing on it. I stop in the parking lot and go inside with my order number. The man behind the desk in the office tells me, in a very unfriendly way, that they do not have an order number like the one I have. He tells me I should be at Lester Towel Distributing, and this is George Towel Distributing. Well, excuse me.

"Where is good ol' Lester's place?" I asked. He sort of grunts and says, "It's across the street." Lester doesn't have a sign in front of his place. I think to save money, they only put one sign up. I go across the street and find George and Lester are brothers because they have the same disposition. They both suffer from the grumpies but only Lester has a beard. It takes them about an hour and a half to put the assorted veggies on the truck.

In the meantime, I call my wife from a phone cubicle in the middle of the parking lot in the rain. It is hard to get out of the rain when you only have a two-foot by three-foot aluminum phone holder to hide under. I make the conversation as short as I can, telling my wife I am down to my last shirt, my last pair of Levis, and my last socks and that I have only one more pair of undies. When I shower next it will be the last of what I brought with me unless I buy more clothes somewhere. I am not domestic enough to do clothes washing on the road because it has an air of permanence to it. I have a closet full at home. That makes me sad. I want to be at home putting lip lock on my sweetie and putting on clean clothes. I often wonder how many other truck drivers get themselves into this situation. Running out of anything clean to wear and one thousand miles from home, in the middle of a swamp with alligators and stuff.

One hell of a life, isn't it? Well, as they say, "somebody has to do it." This is the sad part, and if you want to cry, that's okay. If you do, get your hanky out because tears will make the ink run and will make this book hard to read.

Now loaded with assorted veggies from ol' Lester's place, I head to my next destination to get another load. I asked a driver on the CB how to get to Ft. Pierce and how far it is. He tells me the highway, and that it is about one hundred miles. I drive until I come to a roadside park, which should be only fifteen or twenty miles from Fort Pierce, and go to sleep.

Friday morning, April 5th. I get up and drive into Ft. Pierce to get a cup of coffee and a pack of cigarettes. I get to Morton and Son to load at ten minutes until 8:00 a.m. A produce house with people who are not suffering from the grouches. What will they think of next? Maybe it is early yet and they have not had time to get a bad attitude.

The forklift driver asked me if I would put the pallets in the truck for him. I think to myself that this is because he is about five foot ten and weighs about three hundred pounds. If he had to get off his machine and do it, we would be here all day. I reach out for one instead of pulling it off the stack and sliding it. The second one I grabbed like that was a big mistake. I knew what I had done wrong when I felt the muscle pop. I felt something snap in the lower left side of my back. I have been a weight lifter on and off for years, and I knew better than to do what I just did. I have pulled a muscle, and this time, I have really done it right.

I finished the job, and I even stacked some extra boxes of grapefruit on top of the pallets for the forklift driver. I could tell I had really hurt myself this time. I am going to be very sore for a while.

Noon Friday, I drive to a 76 Truck Stop in Vero Beach, and I can barely get out of the truck. I take two aspirin and fuel my truck. I go in, take a shower, and stand under the hot water for at least thirty minutes. I eat a very good dinner from their buffet and go lie down for about an hour. I have called the company to tell them I am loaded and asked when this load is to be delivered. They tell me Monday morning in Little Rock, Arkansas. Well, I will be closer to home than in Florida, I think

31

to myself. I'm glad I have until Monday because, the way I feel, it may take me that long to get there. After my little nap, I can barely get out of bed. I take more aspirin and drive to Daytona Beach.

I have never been to Daytona Beach. With the time I have before the appointed delivery date and time, I think to myself, I should stop if I can find a place to park the truck. This is the last week of Spring Break, and the place is full of kids. Highway IA goes right through town, and I feel a little out of place in this truck. Lots of sports cars and kids in swimming suits, if you want to call what some of the girls are wearing swimsuits. They sure don't leave much to the imagination.

I find a place, a service station that is being remodeled, and ask the manager if I can park there for a while. He tells me it would be fine.

I walk across the street to the beach and walk up and down for a few minutes. Maybe walking in the sand will help my back feel better.

I see the biggest bikini in the world. Omar's Tent and Awning Company must have made it. The woman wearing it definitely has a sense of humor. She will gross about three hundred and fifty pounds, maybe more. If she gets into the water, it could cause high tide. I walk around for about thirty or forty minutes and it has not helped my back at all. I am feeling terrible. I go back to the truck and head north on I-95 to Jacksonville.

I get within thirty miles south of Jacksonville, and it is getting dark and starting to rain, and the traffic is unbelievable. A southbound trucker said on the CB that if we are going through town, we had better have a lot of patience because the traffic is backed up for miles. He said, "If I were you guys, I would get off at the next exit where a 76-Truck Stop is and sit for a couple of hours until the traffic lets up a bit." I get off and park because of the way I feel. I don't want to fight traffic and rain right now. I go to sleep for a couple of hours more and when I wake up, I take more aspirin. I would use the brand name, but I would want an endorsement fee, and since my name isn't Bo, they might not want to pay me.

I take the by-pass around Jacksonville, get on I-10 west, and go about fifty more miles. I pull into a small fuel stop next to Hardy's and call home. I eat a Hardy burger and then drive on for about one hundred and fifty miles. I see another 76-Truck Stop and shut it down for the night.

Saturday morning, April 6th. I get up at 5:00 a.m. and go into the café for breakfast and coffee. I take more aspirin and order pancakes. My back is very stiff and very sore this morning. I guess I can either get better or die. The way I feel, it needs to be one or the other real soon.

I drive to Alabama and turn north on Highway 45. Where this road breaks from the interstate, it is narrow and in a slum neighborhood. I am wondering if I have made a mistake. I go about three miles when I see a truck coming toward me. I ask, "How is the road to Meridian, Mississippi?" He tells me it is fine and to have a good ride. Now I feel a little better and start looking around at the scenery.

Some of the houses along the highway are old-looking, and I wonder if they were here during the Civil War. I pass by a Confederate cemetery with about seventy-five graves in it. My mind wanders back in time and I am looking at the area as if it were 1863. I wonder what the area looked like back then. Were any of these houses here? What about this road, not paved of course, but just a road, a wagon road? I wonder where the soldiers were killed who were buried in that cemetery. Was this a battleground, or were they ambushed along this road? I have always been interested in the Civil War. I believe the reason for my interest is because it doesn't seem possible for our country to have fought each other in that way.

I don't pretend to know all the reasons for one man's hate of another man because of the color of his skin. I don't pretend to know why a man would want to kill another because of this reason or for any other reason for that matter. I am not naive enough to think that all the things we humans do have a reason behind it. What I have a hard time with is how one group of folks would want to kill another group of folks just because of the way they think. I also have a hard time understanding why one human would want to own another human. Maybe that's why we have in our language the word inhumane. But that was a long time ago, and I wasn't there to try to understand those things.

I don't think inhumane is the right word. I don't believe the lower life forms would rip off an old lady's social security check or lie, cheat, steal, or become a politician. Now, that is a bit philosophical for a truck driver. I had better get down off this soapbox before I fall and hurt my back worse than it already is. Back to the driving of the big trucks, for that is what this writing is about, right?

I am sleepy again. I don't think I slept well last night; my back is hurting too much. I see a small "pull off" and sleep for about an hour and a half. I am stiff, but I don't hurt as bad as I did this morning.

I drive on to Jackson, Mississippi, and try to find a truck stop. Going through town I don't see any of the major truck stops that I am used to staying at. I had seen a sign on the other side of town that said something about a truck stop. I wonder where it is. I get on the CB and ask. A guy is talking on his CB radio that must have a thousand watts of power because I have heard him the last fifteen miles. I can't get a word in edgewise. "Excuse me, but if you shut up for just one minute, I might be able to find out where the truck stop is here in Jackson." After telling me about the truck stop, he let me know he was just causing a little hate and discontent on the radio. *"Thank you, and now go ahead and cause all the hate and discontent you want to,"* I thought to myself. *"give 'em hell if you want to, put a meltdown on 'em, for I have the info I need."* Now, is that the proper Christian attitude? I will take two more aspirin and ponder that later. Right now, the truck needs fuel and the body needs fuel, and I have found the truck stop.

They wash my truck with the fill-up. *Well, how about that, a free wash,* I think to myself. My first impression of this place was not what it was after investigation. Not bad. Very clean with a nice café and good chicken fried steak. So much for first impressions.

After putting a lip lock on the chicken fried steak, I call my oldest son Roger, who lives in the Texas panhandle. A driver can go just so long without finding out how the grandkids are, you know. They are just fine and my son tells me about getting a phone call wanting to know if he would be interested in going to Kuwait as a diesel mechanic for a construction company. I tell him to check it out and let me know. For what they would pay him, it might be worth going for a while.

It's Saturday evening at 9:00 p.m. I don't think I will go any further today. It is less than three hundred miles to Little Rock, and I can make it tomorrow with enough time to get a good night's sleep before unloading on Monday morning. I also hope I will feel better tomorrow. I am going to get some sleep tonight whether it hair lips the Governor.

Sunday, April 7th. I left Jackson and went to Vicksburg, then on into Louisiana, where I turned north on Highway 65, which goes through Pine Bluff, and then on to Little Rock, Arkansas. I stopped for lunch at a little truck stop with a café which was on the side of the highway. I really had a good buffet lunch. Excellent cuisine, it could be because it was Sunday. Anyway, it was very good.

Truckers don't say cuisine. They say they are going to stop for a bite to eat. Then, at the "all-you-can-eat buffet," they consume enough food to supply a small, starving African nation for a week. Texas cowboys often chow down while the English indulge in a bit of pleasant repast. I just can't resist poking fun at us humans. We all eat and call it so many different things.

The little store next to the café had baseball caps for two dollars and ninety-eight cents each. I bought one in black with the words "American by Birth—Southern by the Grace of God" on the front. That is cute, don't you think? I wonder if I wear it in Albuquerque, how many natives will be angered by it. We shall see.

I get to Pine Bluff and see a Sears store located in a shopping center. The parking lot has plenty of room, so I park and go shopping for clothes. I find a pair of Levi's, a shirt, some socks, and more Fruit of the Looms, in colors. These new undies have given me a whole new outlook on life. How easily we are swayed from holding to our traditions. I spent forty-seven dollars, and I know washing clothes would have been less expensive. But as I have said, I'm not very domestic and this was easy compared to finding a suitable place for clothes washing and then taking the time to do that little chore.

I hate the word chore because when I was young, I would go see some cousins of mine who lived in southwestern Oklahoma. Before we could do anything, their mother made them do their chores. I have often wondered why she didn't ask them to just feed the chickens instead of doing their chores. Feeding the chickens sounded like such a simple task, but doing the chores sounded like a lot of work. When my brother and I went to see these cousins, work was not what we had in mind.

We just wanted the chickens to be fed and then the girls to be chased.

I get into Little Rock and park across the street from B&R's office. It is on a dead-end street, so this will not cause any trouble or grief for anyone. I have four drops to get unloaded tomorrow. I would like to be unloaded by 1:00 p.m., but I don't think that will happen. The company is supposed to have three of the new Kenworths in, along with new trailers. I was supposed to get one when I started this little adventure. We shall see.

Monday, April 8th. I get to the first stop off, and I am at the second one before 8:30 am. At the second food company, they tell me they are training a new receiver. Something tells me this could be trouble. The old receiver tells me my unloading appointment is not until 10:30, and they have four trucks unloading now. He went on to explain that this number of trucks is all the new guy can handle at one time. From what I can see, one truck may be more than he can handle at one time. I will have patience and wait until 10:30. At noon I ask the new receiver what about my unloading appointment at 10:30? He tells me he was told I didn't have an appointment and to unload me last. In a sort of unfriendly way, I show him on his unloading schedule that it clearly shows that at 10:30 a.m. I am the appointed one to unload. What can I say, the first day on the job, give him a break, right? After lunch, they start to unload my truck.

I think that I have ceased to enjoy my stay at Quality Foods. If they want this stuff, they had better get on the stick, or I might just take this garbage down the road and sell it to the homeless on the street. Couldn't you see a bunch of bag ladies selling cucumbers, radishes, squash, and eggplants from their shopping carts on the street? I hate myself for the thought of it. Anyway, they have started to unload the veggies now. I have hired a lumper to separate it. Produce has to be separated according to its kind. They don't want the eggplants and the yellow squash on the same pallet. I think George Bush may be right about some of this stuff.

The lumper gets the stuff off the truck, and I hire him to go to the last two stops with me and unload the rest of the trailer. This will cost me (the company) fifty dollars. My company is not as frugal as Navajo Freight about their unloading costs.

At the last stop, I called the office to ask about the load to California and whether the new trucks had come in. There is a stall from the dispatcher, and he tells me to come back to the office when I get empty. I hear something in his voice that tells me something is rotten in Little Rock, and it is not the eggplants. I get unloaded, pay the lumper, and head for the office.

I am beginning to think there is a conspiracy against my going home to see my wife. They, the trucking company, seem to know when you want to go home and will do everything possible to keep you out here on the road far away from home. I can't understand what I have done to them for this kind of treatment. I think to myself that I should take aspirin and cure this, but taking a six-pack of Coors may be better medicine unless they have a load leaving for California tonight.

Monday 4:30 p.m. I get to the office and find out the new Kenworth trucks have not arrived. I know from much experience in the business world that most employers use the Mushroom method when giving information to their employees. The Mushroom method is to keep them in the dark and feed them full of Bull Shit. But in the trucking industry, this odious substance flows like water from a fire truck.

Jerry, the dispatcher, tells me this sad story. I am the only truck in town, and they have this hot load of—guess what—ice cream, and I am the only one who can take it. "Anyway, the new trucks are not here, and you would not want to be in California when they come in, now would you?" he says. Right now, I'm not sure I would mind taking a '49 Ford to California. "Well, I'm easy; where does this stuff go?" I asked. Atlanta, Georgia, is the answer. I could have guessed as much. He tells me this will pay very well, and I say, "Okay, I guess." I catch the safety man who hired me and tell him I think they should get their poop together and in one sack. He agrees with me and says they will make it up to me in the future. I am getting a bad taste in my mouth again. Jerry gives me the dispatch, and I have got to be in Sikeston, Missouri, at 9:00 p.m. to load.

Chapter Four

Monday 9:15 p.m. Sikeston, Missouri. I got here at nine, even though it was supposed to be a five-hour drive, and I left Little Rock at 5 pm. I am just a hammer-down kind of guy. The shipping clerk and dockworker are one and the same at night. He tells me that out of the twenty-four pallets on my trailer, eighteen are not good enough to take, and I will be charged eight dollars each for them. Well, I am not a happy camper. I call the dispatcher and tell him if I am to be charged for the refused pallets, I will bring the truck back to Little Rock and they can get another driver for the ice cream. I can catch a plane to Albuquerque. The quick response was, "Oh no, you won't be charged for them; we will pay it because we are having a real hard time with the ice cream company and our pallets." With that cleared up, I get my frozen goodies and head out while telling the shipping clerk/dock worker to have a nice night.

If this were a fiction novel, it would be right about now that the plot thickens, but since it is nonfiction, it is where the poo-poo hits the fan. Murphy strikes again, hard.

I go east in the direction of Kentucky, and after about an hour, I pull over for a pit stop. I checked the reefer temperature, which for ice cream should be kept at twenty below zero.

I have a theory about why the temperature needs to be kept at twenty below zero. You see if the Mickey Mouse Bars are frozen very hard, they will stay in the mouth and between the bicuspids for a longer period of time so as not to freeze the innards of the young tyke who is eating this sugary substance. The longer it stays in the mouth, the longer the harmful tooth-decaying agents have to work on the little guy's teeth. Now, numerous dental students are studying and plotting the assassination of guys like Dr. Redd Duke for telling us not to eat so much of this stuff that is bad for us. You see these dental students are like the young medical student I had as a bank customer a few years ago. He wore a shirt that read, "I am going to be a Doctor." On his bicycle was a license plate that read, "I am going to be a Mercedes Benz."

I am not so sure we should take to heart all that Dr. Redd Duke is telling us about our health anyway. We are getting health information from a Texas cowboy with manure on his boots, who is skinny, red-headed, and freckled, who will probably get skin cancer and strains all he eats through facial hair. This same Dr. Red Duke is also the head of the Health Science Center in Houston, Texas.

Well, the temperature is not at twenty below zero. It is ten above zero, and the reefer is having a runaway. It is going into the defrost cycle about every eight to ten seconds. It should go into this defrost cycle about every hour, at twenty below. When I got to Sikeston the inside temperature of the trailer was eighteen degrees below zero, and the ice cream at the plant is kept at twenty below. So, if the reefer doesn't quit completely, the ice cream should be alright when I get to Atlanta.

I check the temperature again as I go through Nashville. I stop just long enough to look at the reefer because the light that would allow me to monitor the temperature from inside the cab is out, and at night, I can't see it. I put the pedal to the metal as they say and don't stop again until I am about twenty miles from Atlanta. The temperature is up to twelve above now, but I think it will be okay.

I get backed into the dock at 9:10 a.m., and the receiver checks the ice cream in at fourteen below zero. That is acceptable; anything within a few degrees either way from fifteen or below is acceptable.

I call in and tell the dispatcher of the problem. He tells me not to tell the people there at United Refrigeration. I asked Jerry if he thinks these people who unload ice cream all day, five days a week, are stupid. They asked me when they opened their door and looked at the inside of my trailer if I had a problem. I told them what it was, and they checked the temperature of the ice cream, and it was okay. At twenty degrees below zero, the inside of the trailer would have a thick layer of frost on it.

I told Jerry, "Had I told those guys nothing was wrong, they would have known I was not being honest with them." "Jerry," I said, "Use your head. It's the only thing that makes you smarter than the monkeys." I am not sure he even noticed I had just insulted him. Dispatchers don't need to be real smart; they just need to be good liars. They should learn that sometimes it is better to tell the truth.

I am scheduled to reload in the same door, number seventy-seven at eleven this morning. The dispatcher tells me to take the trailer to Thermo King and get it fixed. I call Thermo King, and they are on the other side of Atlanta. It must be thirty miles or more. I get there and get it fixed. It was the defroster module that had gone bad.

I sleep for a half-hour while at Thermo King, then go back to United Refrigeration. I get there at 3:30 p.m., and just as I pull into their parking lot, I hear the reefer engine making an unusual noise. I am trying to precool the trailer to twenty below. The damn thing is running out of diesel fuel.

The fuel in the reefer tank on this particular trailer should last about forty to forty-eight hours, running at a normal speed. With the defroster coming on every ten seconds, I guess it used all the fuel in about fourteen hours. I call in and tell the dispatcher, then head for a fuel stop which is about six miles away. I get the tank filled and try to start the engine. Diesels are very hard to start if they have run out of fuel. I am hoping I caught it in time and shut it off before it ran completely out. It starts. I have lucked out, I guess.

I have been awake since 5 a.m. yesterday morning, running on just half an hour of sleep, and it hasn't exactly been a fun-filled day. It's becoming a downpour now as I go back to United Refrigeration to load more ice cream going to Deerfield Beach, Florida. I get backed into the dock at 4:30 p.m., and it takes them at least an hour to load the trailer.

I sleep until one of the shipper's hammers on the door of the truck. "You are loaded," he says. It is 6:00 pm now, and I am supposed to be in Deerfield Beach at seven in the morning. I don't think I can make it, but I think I will try, just to surprise the dispatcher. It is just six hundred miles from here, nothing that a real stepper couldn't do. But I only have a sixty-five-mile-an-hour truck. Hmm. So, I better get it in gear, I think to myself. Nevertheless, first things first. I go to the TA Truck Stop in Atlanta, fuel the truck, fuel the belly, wash the body, call my wife, and then cut out across the hot sand dunes or something similar, like pine trees and asphalt.

I get just south of Macon, Georgia, and run into a storm, a thundershower of great magnitude. The wind is coming out of the southwest at thirty to forty miles per hour, and the rain is coming down in sheets. Damn, I'm tired, and I just heard on the CB about a truck that the wind has blown over. It can't be more than a couple of miles away from where I'm at. The ice cream is heavy, and the total truck, trailer, and ice cream weigh in at about seventy-six thousand pounds. I shouldn't have to worry about the wind unless it gets a lot stronger than it is now.

I am on I-75, and just as I cross into Florida, there is an agricultural inspection station. Most reefer trucks coming into Florida, unless they are carrying meat, would have their reefer units shut off. The officer asked, "What are you carrying?" "Ice cream," I tell him. He tells me to pull over and bring in my papers. I take them in, and they look them over. "Okay," he says. I see some boxes of M and M's on his desk with a note under them. It says they are fifty cents, and it is for the officer's son and his little league baseball team. I walk out, munching on the chocolate goodies, leaving the AG officer with a smile on his face.

I drive the rest of the night and get to Deerfield Beach, Florida, only minutes later than the appointed time for delivery. They only take one hour to unload all the ice cream.

This is the cleanest food distribution warehouse I have ever seen. Publix Food Distribution must be new from the way the place looks. They even have a cute spiral staircase leading to a second-floor walkway that crosses the trucking driveway. Nice. This way the employees are not in competition with the trucks coming in and out. There is not even a leaf of lettuce lying on the ground next to the building. Not only are they very clean, but they are also the fastest I have ever seen. The receivers come out to the truck, wake me when they are finished unloading, and hand me the signed bills of lading. I wish they were all like this place. They even have smiles on their faces. They must have one hell of a union here. If all the food distribution warehouses were like this one, there would be at least five thousand guys wanting my job. I don't have anything to worry about, because they are not all like this one. As I have said, one of the job descriptions for receivers is to make the truck driver's life miserable whenever possible. These guys here are very young. In a few years, they might become like all the rest. I think it is from being in a frozen food locker all day when the rest of the world is out in the sunshine, wearing shorts.

I call the dispatcher and tell him where I am and that I am empty. I am not sure he believes me at first. He tells me to take a nap for an hour or two and call him. "Jerry, I have been up for two days and nights. I don't think one or two hours will heal me up. I will call in when I wake up if it is before five this afternoon." I said that to give him grief. I doubt I will sleep over five or six hours at the most. From experience, I have learned that in a produce area such as Florida, when a truck does not make this run regularly, it takes them a while to find a load. I have also learned that as long as the dispatcher gets a good night's sleep, he is not overly concerned about my sleep or loss of same.

I am told there is a motel about a mile from here with a large parking lot, and they don't mind if a truck parks there for a while. I call in at 2:00 pm after sleeping for five hours. Now, they are not in as big of a hurry as they said this morning. They tell me they are working on a produce load and I should get a good night's sleep and call them in the morning. Dispatchers are funny that way. In a hurry, then not in a hurry. I think in their job training; they are put in a tank full of bovine residue and then told to tell the driver to call back in an hour. They lose all perspective of time except for potty time, lunchtime, and quitting time.

Chapter Five

I unhook from my trailer and drive to the beach, which is only a couple of miles from the motel where I parked. There is a large parking lot across the street from the beach, and it doesn't have any signs that say no truck parking. I park the truck, walk to the beach, and look around. Most of the people here are of the gray and retired type. Not many young people are even in the water. This must be a retirement town for the most part. I decide to stay for a while, go back to the truck, and change into my shorts. I want to walk along the water's edge barefoot and get sand in between my toes. Even truck drivers go for the gusto whenever possible.

There is a fishing pier about one-fourth of a mile to the north of the parking lot. I walk down the beach to the entrance and there is a café that serves clam strips. I get an order and look out over the Atlantic while eating. I hear a guy at the little bait shop next to the café telling another fellow that the fishing has been very slow this afternoon. I was going to rent a pole and try my luck until I heard that bit of bad news. It would have cost me twenty dollars to find that out for myself.

There is a fire station next to the parking lot with a public phone out front, and I call home. One of the firemen from the station came out to the sidewalk and asked me if I was going to stay for the parade. "I didn't know there was to be one," I remarked. "Every evening about this time, the parade starts," he says. I decide to hang around to see what he is talking about.

The street is one way going south for about a mile. Around 6:00 p.m., the traffic gets really heavy. *"This must be the parade the fireman was telling me about,"* I thought to myself. People getting off work, kids from school, and lots of older people. Most of the older people are driving big cars that have New York or Illinois license plates on them.

The fireman tells me he is also a paramedic, and they get about four calls per shift for heart failure. With the number of old people, I see why. I believe they will have a good supply for a long time to come.

The hot topic of conversation on this beach is social security and pension checks. Bikinis are not as much the rage here as canes and support hose. Hearing aids are in style on this beach, and orthopedic swimwear is another hot item. At Deerfield Beach, blondes don't have more fun; they have all turned gray, or their hair has fallen out altogether.

Thursday, April 11th. I have slept seven hours, and I feel better, to say the least. I get up and go into the Denny's which is on the corner in front of the motel. I order breakfast and have coffee. As I look around, I notice something very unusual. Every woman in here who looks as if they are under the age of thirty is with a man who looks to be over sixty. This must be the sugar daddy capital of Florida. We certainly don't believe this is National Secretary Week, and these guys are taking their young secretaries out for breakfast, now do we?

These guys probably call their wives and say I have got to go to Florida for a couple of days on business. Do you think the little woman knows what kind of business, or monkey business, he does in Florida? Hell, yes, because she just got off the phone with her tennis teacher and told him the hubby has gone to Florida, so come on over and bring your toothbrush.

I knew a guy this happened to. His wife then married the tennis coach, and he married a cute little French teacher who was at least twenty-five years his junior.

I have a theory that ex-wives do not grow old gracefully; they get ugly during the divorce. Even more so if the ex-wife has an attorney who personally does not like the ex-husband. Some ex-wives try to lose thirty or forty pounds after the divorce, so they stand a better chance of catching another poor fool. When they catch this guy, they gain the forty pounds back, dye their hair, and always put on too much makeup.

If there was a scientific study done, I think they would find them to be cousins of the female Black Widow Spider. Always larger than their hubbies and meaner than a snake.

The humidity yesterday didn't seem too bad until the evening. As night approached, the humidity pegged the needle. Potato chips melt in your hand, not in your mouth. Wilting must be a common disorder here in Florida. I knew a cowboy from Oklahoma who said he suffered from dropsy, but I think wilting might be worse.

I have just called the office, and they want me to call back in an hour. There are two phone booths next to the 7-11 stores, and before I started to dial the office, the other phone rang. I answered it, and the voice asked if Bill was in. I said he was out just now but to call him back later, for I was sure he would be in. This guy will go home tonight and tell his wife that Bill needs to get a mobile phone because he is never in his office. It is amazing how much fun you can have trucking.

Truck drivers sometimes don't say what they mean. When a driver says on the CB, he has a tire getting hot, that means he is going to pull over for a pit stop. He says, "I am going to ease on down to Miami," then passes you doing eighty-five with his window down. This causes the fire from his cigarette to fall on his arm, causing a burn. When he gets to a truck stop, he is rubbing his arm and telling the guys how bad the trucking business has gotten. This guy usually has hemorrhoids and gingivitis.

It is now 1:00 pm, and I have driven south of Miami on Highway 1 to Homestead, Florida. I was not sure there was a place in the United States that had stranger people and sights than in Albuquerque, New Mexico, but I may have found it here in Homestead. Some strange things are basking in the sunshine here. I was walking across the parking lot of a Winn-Dixie supermarket when I saw a little white French Poodle running sideways. Its forward progress was in the direction of Georgia, but its head was aimed toward the Atlantic Ocean, and its rear end was headed for the Gulf of Mexico. I think I will ponder what might cause such a disorder over lunch. With a little training, the owner could get the dog on the Johnny Carson Show or at least David Letterman.

At noon, I walked across the highway to eat at a McDonalds. When I walked in, there was a line of people darn near the front door, waiting to place their orders. After what seemed a frightfully long time, I finally made it to the counter to place my order. I said in a weak voice, extreme hunger makes my voice weak, "I think you could use some Mc Help. Is this the home of the Whopper?" This extremely large and nondomestic woman, who was standing behind the counter, did not see the humor in my statement. If looks could kill, I would have received my Mc Burger posthumously. I then did what any red-blooded guy of my stature would have done under similar circumstances. I grabbed my Mc Fries and made a hasty retreat from the reach of this gigantic Mc Person.

While I was enjoying this long wait in line, I spied a young man with an advertisement on his shirt that read, "City of Homestead." I asked him where this metropolis started, and where did it end? I didn't even know I had arrived until I saw the sign: Homestead Buick. I asked if the city fathers wanted travelers to know the whereabouts of this place. He just shrugged his shoulders. I think he is still pondering the question.

I went back to Winn-Dixie to get a banana for dessert. Looking at palm trees has this effect on me sometimes. I got into the checkout line that was designated ten items or less, cash only. There was only one person in front of me. Before I paid for the banana, it had ripened considerably. I'm not saying all the people here are slow, only the ones who are not driving a car. The people are driving like they are running from the cops, except this one couple from Ontario, Canada. I managed to get stuck behind them for most of five miles on the way here. Everyone else was flying, sixty-five or more. These folks of foreign extraction must have been lost because they were buzzing right along at thirty-five. I have seen two other cars from Ontario, Canada, on this journey, and they all seem to have a calling for the obstruction of traffic.

I call the dispatcher from a public phone in front of the Winn-Dixie, and I go on the "call me back in an hour program again and again."

A man who works for the supermarket comes out the door and sits down on a bench that is against the wall. He lights a cigarette and I walk over and also sit down. "What is the principal industry in this area," I asked. "Farming," he explains. "Oh, there must be a lot of people from Cuba around here," I said. "No, they won't do farm work. The Cuban people are mostly in Miami and doing well," he explained. "We have a lot of Mexicans doing the farm work."

I said, "I can understand that. I bet there is more money in cocaine than there is in picking tomatoes." Well, I think I have managed to insult another Floridian because he promptly got up and went back into the store. These people are sure touchy about this place.

My last call to the dispatcher was successful—they have found a load for me to pick up.

I have now gone to the Farmers Market in Florida City. It is a complex with many produce companies. The one where I am to load is in the middle of the complex. It's crowded in here, and not much room to get a truck as long as mine backed into the dock. I get it in with the tractor at a forty-five-degree angle to the trailer. Now, if another truck needs to get by me, he won't take part of my front end with him. The people running this place are very nice. One even has a big sign behind his desk that reads, "Do it with Jesus." The Towel brothers could learn something from these folks.

Most of the truck drivers have a look on their faces that reads, "How did I find this place, and how do I get out once I get in."

I have loaded the produce and am told by Jerry my next stop is Immokalee, Florida. I find it on the map and it is on the other side of the Everglades. This drive should be interesting, to say the least. I head north on State Highway 997 to Highway 41, where I turn west into the Everglades.

The two-lane highway is narrow, and my truck and trailer are not. Each side of the road is ten feet wide, and this trailer is eight- and one-half feet wide. This does not leave much room for error. At fifty-five miles an hour, meeting another truck going fifty-five miles an hour is like going down a lane with eighteen inches of margin and moving at one hundred ten miles an hour. For the sake of math students, that is about eighty-eight feet per second. Now, to top this off, there are trees within one foot of the asphalt that are forty feet tall. They have trimmed the branches to where a trailer that is thirteen- and one-half feet tall can barely clear. Meeting an oncoming truck gets a little tense, to say the least, especially when you are also talking on the CB and looking at the fourteen gauges on the dash, unwrapping a package of cheese crackers, and sipping an RC at the same time. It's no wonder they call us professional drivers.

Dale Earnhardt should try this. Dale drives a car that is sixteen feet long, less than six feet wide, and weighs less than two tons. These big trucks average sixty-five feet long, eight feet wide, thirteen and a half feet high, and weigh forty tons. The engine in Dale's car has 350 Cubic Inch Displacement, and the horsepower is like a thoroughbred horse: fast but needs lots of care. The truck engine has an average of 850 Cubic Inch Displacement, and many have over 400 draft horse type horsepower. The race car has four gears, where the truck can have as many as eighteen gears, some have even more.

Once, during this part of the drive, I passed a cab over Kenworth, and I knew there were not over three inches between our mirrors when we met. This would not be a drive for the trainee truck driver or those with a weak heart.

After about ten miles of driving in this tree tunnel, the scenery started to open up. There were fewer trees along the highway. The trees had been replaced with water. In Texas, these would be called bar ditches. They looked like canals to me. Then I saw it! It was on the rocks along the canal's bank. I think this is the first alligator I have ever seen in the wild. The darn critter looks to be ten to twelve feet long, with his mouth open. In the next twenty miles, I count over fifteen of these swamp critters that I later find has the nickname "Wally."

This type of drive will give a person a stiff neck from tension. Driving fifty-five to sixty-five on this narrow highway, looking for alligators and other critters, and wanting to get to my destination in one piece is definitely a challenge. I once thought vice presidents in banks were underpaid for the conditions. You know, paper cuts and all the other hazards of the job. If the potential for danger was a criterion for salary, right now, I should be making over one hundred dollars per hour. Dream on, fool.

I have also seen many large turtles along this road and two raccoons looking like they were fishing. I turned north for the town of Immokalee on Highway 29. This road is no better than the last one.

I have seen a few people fishing along the roadway. One was pulling in a good-sized fish. I wish I had the time to stop and see what they were catching. There is no place to get a truck of this size off the road. I passed through an area that had Panther crossing signs. One of these signs was followed by another sign just a few feet away, which read, "Roadside Park Picnic Tables."

In the area, there are alligators, snakes, panthers, and other critters that might pose a threat to human life. I can just imagine some family of tourists from Iowa at this roadside park. The mother says to the little kids who have been cooped up in the car all day, "Kids, don't go too far now, and watch out for snakes." Little does she know they could get bit, eaten, and snacked upon by all sorts of critters.

As I turned the corner onto Highway 29, I saw a fish jumping out of the water, not once but three or four times. I wonder what was under there that was after the fish. I was just wondering. I have no desire to go down there and check it out myself. I figure an alligator fourteen feet in length, with a mouth as big as Fort Worth, and with all those big teeth, is a good deterrent to any desire I might have to go swimming hereabouts.

I get to Immokalee and find the produce house. I go inside their office and have phone calls waiting for me. One is the produce house from Florida City; the other is my dispatcher. The guy from Florida City says they forgot to give me a state inspection paper on the limes I picked up there. He says they will fax me a new manifest without the limes on it. That way, I can try to bootleg the limes out of the State. Okay, no problem, I can handle that.

Next, the dispatcher, who has now been on hold for three or four minutes. He seems unhappy about being on hold even if he would have no problem putting a driver on hold for ten minutes. I just love people like that. He wants to know if I can smuggle the limes out without getting caught. "Hell yes," I tell him, "The stuff ain't dope." I haven't seen any lime-sniffing dogs at the inspection stations lately. If the limes are not on the manifest and they don't decide to unload the trailer, and if I don't look too guilty, I might just be able to sneak them through. I go through all this aggravation for a Corona taste enhancer. What a job this is. I could just see it now. I am being sent to prison, and some convict will ask, "What are you in for?" "Smuggling Limes."

"Jerry, there are things for you to worry about, like how to get me a load to the house, correcting your slice on the golf course, or whether you can pay your phone bill this month. But not twenty little boxes of limes in the front of this forty-eight-foot-long trailer that I am going to smuggle out of the State of Florida," I said.

A woman with a clipboard in her hand comes over to me and tells me which door to back my truck into. I get the doors opened and start to get backed into the dock when a guy comes running and waving his arms at me. I stop and ask what he wants. "Your trailer door is swinging, and it almost hit the truck next to you." I go check this out and find the latch that holds the open door up against the trailer has broken. I use a bungee cord to secure it and back into the dock.

I go into the cooler, where the woman with the clipboard is standing. She started telling me it is a state law that green bell peppers cannot be put on pallets on a truck going out of the state. I look her straight in the eyes and ask, "Do I look like I just got off the boat or just fell from a turnip wagon or something? Do I look like this is my first load of produce as a truck driver?" She again tells me this is the law. "The bell peppers will not cool if they are stacked on pallets," she explains. I think I have heard it all now. "Stack them on pallets anyway," I said. "I will take the chance." Why the heck not? I am already smuggling limes. "My boss won't let us do that," she exclaimed.

"Fine with me if that's the way your boss wants it, but don't bull crap me with the state law, and it won't cool stories. I have been hauling bell peppers a long time and on pallets, too." I said.

Two black guys started taking the boxes from the forklift and hand-stacked them on the floor of the trailer. When they were almost finished, the girl with the clipboard asked me if I wanted to tip the forklift driver and the two guys doing the stacking. She explained they would divide it three ways, equally. This woman acts just like my ex-wife, for she doesn't know when to let well enough alone. "I sure do want to give them a tip and you the same tip as well," I said to the woman. "Never try to bull shit the truck drivers, then ask for money from them; it makes them act ugly toward all mankind, especially the ones that work for produce companies." If looks could kill, I should have been a dead man right there in the warehouse.

I go to the office and get the bills for this stuff, then go out to the truck to pull away from the dock, to close my doors. Before I went to the office, I had waited until the forklift driver had put all my pallets back on the truck. Now, in the truck, I start the engine, push in the air parking brake handles, put the truck into first gear, and slowly disengage the clutch. I move away from the dock, far enough to close the trailer doors. As I open the truck door to get out, the forklift driver comes running up to me.

"Why don't you tell someone when you are going to move your truck? I was still in your trailer straightening up your pallets," he yelled. It becomes clear to me these folks just don't understand the trucking business. It may have something to do with smelling bell peppers all day.

"What in the hell were you doing in my trailer? Do you think this is the only place I will ever stop to pick up this kind of garbage? Hell, I am going all of two city blocks to the next garbage house, and the forklift driver is going to take these same pallets off this truck and stack the damn things on the damn dock. Then put more of this same green bell pepper crap on pallets, and put them on my damn truck. Then this same forklift driver is going to put these same pallets back on my damn truck, and he will not spend ten minutes trying to make them look neat."

"Then he will get his ass out of my trailer, and he will not, I repeat, NOT, ask for a damn tip for doing his job." I turn and just walk away, with my arms in the air, in a final gesture of, "Kiss my ass; I've got to go now, thank you very much, and have a nice day."

Some truck drivers, when provoked, will talk this way. Others will express themselves with the use of mild expletives with little or no provocation at all. Some truck drivers talk this way, or worse, almost all the time. Sometimes a good hell or a damn helps to get the point across.

Chapter Six

Friday morning April 12th. I am five miles from Fort Pierce, Florida, at Morton and Son, orange and grapefruit aficionados. I get there as before, at about 7:45 a.m. They tell me when I check in that it will take a while to get my order ready because they have not run the red grapefruit. "About when do they plan to run the red grapefruit?" I asked. "About two this afternoon," she said. "They should have yours ready about 4:00 pm." What fun! I get to sit here all day for three hundred and eighteen boxes of fruit.

I go to the 76-Truck Stop in Vero Beach and take a shower then eat at their buffet. This being Friday, they have fish, and since it is only four or five miles to the Atlantic Ocean, I think it should be good fresh fish. Not bad for a truck stop, but as I may have mentioned this is one of the cleanest and nicest truck stops, I have ever seen.

I also fueled the truck and changed a broken headlight, got my map out of the truck, and gave a driver directions to Belle Glade and the infamous "Towel Distributing Company."

The headlight must be put on a separate billing from the truck fuel. The woman at the fuel counter put the fuel and the headlight together on the company fuel card and then had to redo the whole thing. By the time she had finished, it had taken her longer to do this than the fueling and direction-giving process.

I go back to Morton and Son to wait for the oranges and grapefruit. I decide to ask the girl in the office about the progress of the red grapefruit that hadn't been gathered earlier. When I walk up to the counter the girl hands me a form to fill out. She informs me I must fill this out completely before I can get my order processed. I tell her I had already done this when I was here this morning at 8:00 a.m. "Don't you recognize me? I'm the driver that was wearing the black cap," I said. She then exclaimed, with very big eyes, "You are the guy wearing the black cap and the red shirt."

"You certainly are very observant," I said with a smile, "But you didn't recognize me."

"No, I didn't," she said with a look of surprise. I responded, "No two-day beard, no slightly soiled red shirt, and I have my TV Evangelist hair uncovered by the cap. I can't believe you didn't know me!" The girl's smile got even wider, and she said, "You really look different now, and I'm sorry, but they still don't have your order ready." She sounded almost apologetic.

Well, it's nap time. Nap's over. They came to my truck to tell me they wanted me to go back into door number one - the red grapefruit was ready to load. All this nice treatment because I showered, shaved, put on clean clothes, and my TV preacher hairdo.

The humidity has pegged the needle again this afternoon. A few clouds are coming from the direction of the Atlantic Ocean. It is starting to rain even though the sun is shining. I think I know why the natives of old wore so little clothing in this part of the country. When it rained in the middle of the day, like it is now, they would grab their bar of Ivory and scrub off a little. Whoops, I see a slight problem in that we are now all lathered up with Ivory, and the rain has stopped. Well, that just chaps my hide. No wonder the natives were restless; they have just gaulded themselves. I bet they knew how to make salve back in those days. The chafing may not have been as big a problem as I first envisioned, for it is raining again. Maybe the pause was to let the soap work more efficiently than the way we do this chore now. We put the stuff on, slosh it around a little, and rinse it right off with little or no pause. This may be due to the fact we are always in a hurry to get to our appointed task in life. People in Los Angeles could benefit from this revolutionary way of bathing; it might save water. That is unless they had to wait on the rain, then L. A might have an even worse smell than it does now.

I think I have spotted a graduate of Texas A&M. He is driving a SEX truck (South Eastern Express). He is exhibiting some of the traits that are indigenous to those who have attended Texas A&M University. He is wearing a big black cowboy hat, his shirttail is hanging out, and his Wranglers are tucked into the tops of his Tony Lamas. He has his elbows cocked back, and his forefingers are touching his thumbs. This is the way real cowboys walk. He walks as if his hemorrhoids have bothered him for a very long time. Classic "Aggie" if I ever saw one, and I have seen one or two. I once knew a bank president from the Texas Panhandle who was an "Aggie." This guy was reported to wear purple jockey shorts and purple socks every day.

It's now 4:30 p.m., and I got here at 7:30 a.m. I always like spending the whole day loading three hundred eighteen boxes of fruit. I think they must feel sorry for me now because they are using two forklifts to load the stuff. The next to the last pallet is put on the trailer by the new forklift driver, and with one of the forks, he gouges a foot-long hole inside of my trailer. I am standing right there, and as soon as he backs out of the trailer, I point this out to him. He gets in a panic, runs over to the other forklift driver, and tells him of his error. The general manager and my company talk on the phone, get the proper insurance information, and got the last pallet of grapefruit loaded. Sometimes, there is pain and anguish associated with loading grapefruit.

It is now 6:00 p.m., and I head back to the truck stop at Vero Beach. Because of the delay in getting the grapefruit, I cannot get the rest of the load until tomorrow. Two more loads to pick up. My first stop is in a town called Frost Proof; the last one is in Apopka, which I find on the map to be just north of Orlando. Frost Proof is straight west of here, about seventy-five miles. From looking at the map, the way to get there is on Highway 60, which crosses the Okeechobee Swamp. I think I will stay here until tomorrow morning and then go to Frost Proof.

I walk around in the truck stop for a few minutes until I get bored and ask a man who is at the cash register if he has ever been on Highway 60. He tells me it is a good road, but narrow, with swamp on both sides. In fog conditions, there have been some very bad wrecks on that road. I've always liked to hear words of encouragement after a long and almost fruitless day, except for the three hundred and eighteen boxes of grapefruit, which I finally managed to get on my truck. I think it might be better to get across the swamp today rather than take a chance on there being fog out there early in the morning.

I grab a couple of ham and cheese sandwiches and a Coke from the cooler and go back to my truck. As I eat the sandwiches and think over my options, I decide to go on today. Besides, I won't need to be in a hurry, and there may be someone fishing along the road. If there would be a place to get the truck off the roadway, I could see what they are catching, and watch for a while. Yep, that's the plan; I gobble down the goodies and head west on Highway 60.

I go about fifteen miles and come to a bridge that is allowing the swamp water on the left side of the road to mingle with that on the right. There is a white Toyota pickup parked on the left side of the bridge, and I see two fellows fishing. This is falling right into my plans if I can park the truck off the roadway. I stopped and found there was plenty of room to park at the side of the road. I set the parking brakes and get out. I go across the highway, walk up to the two guys and said, "How you guys doing today. What are you fishing for?"

"Wally," was the reply. With a puzzled look on my face, I asked, "What kind of fish is a "Wally?"

"No man, Wally ain't no fish," he replied, "We're fishing for Wally Gator." With an equally puzzled look, I said, "Alligators! You're fishing for Alligators?"

The rod and reel the guy was using was what I would use for bass fishing. For bait, they were using what looked to me like a topwater bass plug. The line on the reel didn't look to be any different than I would use. "That line can't be more than a fourteen-pound test. You aren't going to catch a very big Gator using that," I exclaimed.

"That's all we need 'cause when the Gator comes up and bites the lure, I shoot him in the head with this." The one doing the talking then pulled from under his shirt a 22-caliber semi-automatic pistol. "Then we drag him into the bank."

"Interesting," I thought to myself, so I asked the guys, "How much can you get for an Alligator hide these days?"

The reply was, "Oh, about three to five years in the state pen. But we don't want the hides; we are just after the meat. We throw the rest back." I start thinking that, if caught, I could get into deep poo-poo for just being here.

About that time a five-foot Alligator comes to the surface not ten feet from the shore. "There's Wally," one of the guys shouted. I saw him, and that convinced me it was time I was moving along.

"Hey, good luck with your fishing. I got to be going," I said as I started back across the highway to my truck for a hasty getaway. I take off like the cops were after me and looked in the mirrors just to make sure they weren't.

As I head down the road, I notice the area is not as swampy as I thought it would be. These are ranch lands of sorts. There are some of the mangiest looking cow critters I have ever seen, this side of New Mexico, grazing in these pastures. They all look like high-speed bovines. It could be to get away from their adversaries—alligators and such—that might be hiding in the bushes in these parts.

I go west on Highway 60 for about another ten miles and come to a highway intersection with a four-way stop. This is the first sign of civilization, except for the gator fishermen I have seen since I left the truck stop. There is a convenience store, a couple of service stations, and one or two assorted empty buildings before I get to the stop sign at the crossroads. On the northwest corner of the intersection is an old and rustic looking building, with a red neon sign in the front that reads, "Yeehaw Junction Bar and Grille." After all of the fun I've just had, I think it is time for a cup of coffee. I park the truck in front of an abandoned service station across the street and go into the "Yeehaw Junction Bar and Grille."

Chapter Seven

There are eight or ten cars parked in front and a couple of trucks along the road. I step inside and notice it is only about six and a half feet from ceiling to floor. There are about fifteen tables, all with white tablecloths on them. The bar is three-sided, with four or five bar stools per side. Behind the bar are shelves with assorted bottles of liquor, some with more dust than others.

In the right corner of the room, before the entrance to the restrooms, stand wooden Indians about four feet high. On the walls are a hodgepodge of pictures, snake skins, and stuffed fish. One of the pictures is of an alligator.

Sitting on a stool in front of the wooden Native Americans, a guy is playing an electric guitar and singing Country and Western songs. Now, I don't mean attempting to sing, I mean with Nashville, Grand Ole Opry quality. This guy ain't no amateur. From the way he sounds, he is definitely a professional. I hop up on one of the barstools to listen and order a cup of coffee.

The waitress, who is also the owner, walks over and says, "What are you gonna have?" This woman is built like Dolly Parton, on top as well as on the bottom. There is a lot of waitresses here.

"Do you folks discriminate against tall people?" I asked. She laughed and said, "No, but when this place was built, they might have."

"Ma'am, I think I will have a cup of coffee, please." My mother raised me to have manners like that. She looks at me and says, "You a tourist?"

63

"No, ma'am, I drive a truck," I said. "You don't look like no truck driver I ever saw," she exclaimed.

"Well, you see, I have been out here longer than I thought I was going to be, and I have run out of everything to wear except these shorts and this "Hobe" shirt. I really am driving a truck; it's the red Freightliner parked across the road." "The hell you are," she said as she went to get the coffee.

While she was gone to fetch my coffee, I noticed a sign at the top of the liquor cabinet just below glasses shaped like cowboy boots. The sign read "Jackass Juice $2.50." Just below that, another sign read, "Snake Venom $2.00."

When she returns with the coffee, I point at the top sign and asked, "What is in that?" The waitress, grinning, put her elbows on the bar, leaned close to me, and asked, "Are you driving?" "Yes," I answered.

"This is a secret recipe, and I won't sell you one if you're driving because the first one would kick the hell out of you. The second one would make you forget where you are, and you might drive into the swamp."

"What about the Snake Venom," I asked.

"Same thing, secret recipe, not as strong. It just leaves you with the desire to lie down on the floor and hiss. It also makes you immune from snake and alligator bites and attacks from hostile natives," she said. I tell her, "I think I will pass on both; thank you anyway."

As I sip my coffee, I divert my attention back to the music playing in the corner of the room. The singer does four or five more songs, and everyone sure seems to be having a good time listening to his music. On the side of the bar next to the singer, there are eight or nine people all bunched up, clapping and singing with him.

He says he is going to take a break after the next song, which is the theme song for Yeehaw Junction. I am not surprised that this place has its own song, for it is one unusual place. The song starts out "I'm a Heehaw from Yeehaw Junction." Well, I'll be dipped in hog fat and slapped down a rat hole. Darndest place I've ever seen. If I talk like this, maybe they won't think I'm a tourist anymore.

I look around and notice that above each table, suspended by a fishing line, is either a rubber spider or a rubber bat. These critters can be controlled by the person behind the bar. At any time, they can be lowered into your soup. I saw this happen to a couple at one of the tables. They were probably not locals, and when the rubber bat came down, eye to eye with this unsuspecting diner, his mouth lost most of the salad he had put there. Everyone in the place was laughing but him. I thought his wife was going to have a cat, she was laughing so hard. This place definitely knows how to party.

The singer takes his break, comes over to where I am sitting and introduces himself. His name is Danny Johnson, and he has lived here on and off for the past ten years. He is a professional singer with about fifteen years in bars and nightclubs all over the country. He tells me he will never make it to the top that way and has returned to Yeehaw Junction to write his own songs. Someday, he hopes to get a recording contract to do his music. I asked him to sing some of his songs. When he starts again, he does three of the songs he has written, and they are as good as the stuff I hear on the radio. I wonder what kind of luck gets a Ricky Skaggs or Clint Black into the big time because if it is just talent, this guy seems to have plenty of it. This may be the same problem as described by Mark Twain when he said to a group of generals after the civil war: "Greatest general that has ever lived is a shoe cobbler from New Hampshire." The generals replied to this with, "We have never heard of him." Mark Twain then said a very profound thing,

"The reason you never heard of this general is because he wasn't in the Army, and never fought in any war. But if he were in the Army and had fought in the war, he would have gotten more medals than Grant."

I think this is a big problem for most of us. We don't do great things because either we didn't try or were not afforded the opportunity to do them.

About this time a young couple with a little girl about two years old comes in and sits at one of the tables. They talk to Danny Johnson for a few minutes before he goes back to his guitar and his songs. When the woman, who is also pregnant from the way she looks, finishes her salad, Danny says, "Let's get Patty to come up here to sing us a couple of songs." Every one of the regulars who are at the end of the bar start to applaud, and Patty goes up to the microphone. Her first song is "D.I.V.O.R.C.E.," and I think Tammy would have been impressed. She then does a couple of Loretta Lynn songs and sounds just like Loretta. Then she goes back to her table and her order of liver and onions.

I'm starting to feel like "Big Ed of Star Search." I start looking around at the crowd to see who else is here that I might have seen on the Grand Ole Opry. Well, I stay a total of four hours in this café of wonders, and before I went, two more people who play the guitar and sing country music, came in and performed.

All good things must come to an end. I bid everyone a fond farewell and promised if I am ever in these parts again, I will definitely stop in at the Yeehaw Junction Bar and Grille.

Chapter Eight

I drive the forty miles to Frost Proof and find the Frost Proof Growers. It is on the four-lane highway going north and south, Highway 27. I drive into their loading dock area and park for the night. It has been a day to remember, and I am sure that I will.

Saturday morning, April 13th. I wake up at 6:30 a.m. and head across the highway to a convenience store to get some coffee. I asked if there was a café anywhere close that would be open. The cashier pointed to the Frost Proof Growers I just came from and told me their café was open. I am definitely not very observant at 6:30 in the morning, for the café is in the same building I just came from. It is on the highway side, and I was in the back; that may have something to do with my not seeing it. It is a wonder I didn't smell the coffee brewing or the bacon frying. I go back and park in the same spot. I walk around the building, and sure enough, there it is - the café. The place is packed, with only one vacant table. I order a cup of coffee, eggs, bacon, hash browns, and toast. When I went up to pay the check, the total bill was $2.11, American cash. I think this might be a better bargain than an Egg Mc Muffin. Florida is definitely the land of inconsistency.

I am now loaded and leave this haven for cheap food and head north for Orlando and further.

I get to Apopka, Florida, in about an hour and a half. It will take me at least that long again to get through this village of ten thousand poor drivers and residents. I believe the population of this place declined during the time it took me to get through the town.

I almost get to the first intersection in Apopka and see an accident in the middle of the intersection. There is a big shopping center to the right of the street, and this cross street goes into the middle of its parking lots. A motorcycle has hit a car in the side, probably coming out of the mall parking lot or going into it.

There are police cars, sheriff cars, fire trucks, ambulances, fire department emergency vans, and one helicopter all in the street, blocking progress in both directions of the four-lane. There were at least one thousand rubberneckers there to see the death and destruction. From the looks of things, it appears at least one of the riders on the cycle was killed. I think there were two on the bike, but I don't know this for sure. The helicopter took someone away, while one of the ambulances left with another person. One ambulance was still at the scene when I finally got up to the scene of the accident. When the last ambulance left, the officers started letting traffic go on. Neither the bike nor the car was on the four-lane roadway.

The officers were making all the traffic going north turn left at the intersection. I asked the officer why, and he said there had been an accident. I am not sure I could see the logic in this statement, but I turned left. The street went into a residential section and was very narrow. The cop said I could turn right at the first stop sign and get back to the highway. I had to get left, next to the curb, to make the turn, and still almost hit the stop sign with the end of my trailer. I made it to the highway just in time to see two cars hit head-on right in front of me. These people are hell-bent on the destruction of sheet metal and headlights. There is a cop sitting on the north side of the street who sees the whole thing. He is one of the officers who was at the scene of the other wreck. He gets out of his car after turning on his emergency lights and walks over to the new mess.

I asked him if he would hold up traffic going north so I could back up to cross the corner of the service station to my right. I told him I thought it would be a good thing if I could get out of town before one of the "good" drivers in this fine metropolis decides to try to run over my truck while crossing this intersection. He gave me a strange look, but he did as I asked, and I got the heck out of Dodge (Apopka.)

I drive north on Highway 441, trying to find a place where I can get the truck off the road to call the produce company where I am to finish loading the trailer. I spot a used car lot with a tall chain-link fence around it with enough room so I can get my truck off the road. I go up to the door of the office and go in. The owner tells me his office phone is not working but I could go out to his shop and call. After fifteen minutes, I finally had directions, thanked the old man, and drove on.

I was told to turn left at the second stoplight, north of where I called them from, while at the used car lot. I do as I was directed, and the street ends in a matter of a few blocks. I turn left according to the directions and go down this very winding road for about two miles. I turn right and come to a small complex with four or five produce companies.

I get backed into the dock and climb the stairs to the loading platform, where I am met by one of the workers. I go into the office, and we get the order ready. I am to load carrots. These carrots are on pallets. Not the normal pallets but warehouse pallets, whatever they are. I am told they are much larger than the ones I have on my truck. Why not? Everything else here in Florida is out of the ordinary. Why not have odd-size pallets too? I now will have a surplus of eighteen pallets, after I am completely loaded. I tell the supervisor this fact and that I would need to call my company about this pallet issue. After calling my company and explaining the problem, they told me if there is not enough room in the back of my trailer for the remaining pallets, the order of carrots needs to be cut back to allow room for my extra pallets. I told the dock supervisor what my company told me about this load and my extra pallets. A decision was made to use my pallets instead of theirs so all of the carrots could get loaded. Now, even I am getting confused.

Then, a very large black man who works on the dock comes over to me. He tells me they charge two dollars per pallet to restack the pallets, from their large ones to my regular size pallets. Once again, I smell a profit-making deal here, but no profit for me. I say fine, if that's what you charge, go ahead and load the truck.

When they get all the carrots on the truck, there is still room for my pallets that they hadn't used for the carrots. I ask the big guy to help me put them on the trailer. He stands flat-footed and throws them on top of everything. I can't even hold one of the things over my head for three seconds and this guy is tossing them like they were empty cardboard boxes. He should because his neck is larger than my leg. I mean this guy is big, real big.

In the meantime, I have called the dispatcher to tell them I am loaded and headed for Little Rock. I mention the fee for stacking the carrots, to which Jerry tells me the broker pays for us. Okay, that's cool, but who is going to tell that bit of news to this mountain of a man who is throwing the last pallet on my trailer? I tell the supervisor what I have learned about the fees. He simply replies that this is the usual procedure. Hmm, I think to myself, this must make that guy a little extra beer money because he sure is going to want something right now for his trouble. Well, here goes. I walk up to this monster, hand him a five-dollar bill, and say as I am making my get-a-way to the truck, "Thanks for loading the pallets for me; the broker pays for any other fees for us. Have a nice day, and don't spend all that money in one place." If I ever go back there, I can wear a disguise so he won't recognize me.

I head north toward Little Rock and a little bit closer to home. I am about one hundred fifty miles from Apopka when I see another two-car accident on the interstate highway. It amazes me sometimes and hurts my head just trying to figure out why and how two cars could hit each other on a divided four-lane interstate highway. It's the middle of the afternoon, not a cloud in the sky, light traffic, and boom; they smack each other. I wonder if it is the social instinct we humans have that allows this to occur. Or maybe it is the desire for their insurance agents to get to know each other better. I believe a short conversation on the CB radio would suffice. The conversation would go something like get the blank, blank out of my way before I run over you. I know this would have a positive outcome and help the overall economy.

I drive to Atlanta and decide I will go west on I-20 to Birmingham, Alabama. It is almost midnight, and I am tired, but I want to get away from Atlanta so as not to be affected by early morning traffic. I see a small truck stop and decide to stop for the night.

Sunday, April 14th. I head west again on I-20 and pass a lot of signs that say Talladega Race Track. I have gone by the Atlanta track, the one at Darlington and Rockingham, and also in Charlotte. This country is definitely racetrack rich. I have often wondered why there is not more diversification of things like that throughout the whole US of A. We, out west, have most of the Rodeos, and the southeast has all the racetracks. Maybe it's because the southeast had all the rum runners, and the west had all the crazy cowboys. I don't mean goofy crazy, but have you ever considered sitting on a two-thousand-pound bull with a bad disposition? It is more sane, in our society at least, to put the pedal to the metal in the old sedan.

I get to Birmingham and start looking for Highway 78 North. I find the darn thing and find myself winding my way through the whole city. I had a desire to see Birmingham, but not this much of it. I finally get through after an hour of turning this way and that. It is starting to rain as I leave the city.

I go about fifty miles and come to a café on the left side of the highway with a large parking lot. I enjoy a good lunch and go north again in an even harder rain. I have not been listening to the radio and have not heard a weather forecast, but I can make a prediction: heavy rain. There doesn't seem to be any let-up in sight, for the clouds just get heavier the further north I go. I am not fond of two-lane highways, rain, and Sunday drivers. It is a bad combination and could be hazardous to my health.

Sure enough, four of these folks are coming together rather nicely. Right in front of a small country church, too. A four-car smash-up. Looks like one of the cars in this fender bender was leaving the church and hit cars coming in opposite directions. I wondered how they managed that. I believe that if the "dearly beloved" can't drive any better than this, they soon may become the dearly departed. From the size of the church, those involved could reduce the church's Sunday school attendance by half.

I get to the edge of Memphis, Tennessee, and the rain is letting up some. It looks like they have enough rain anyway. Water is standing everywhere. I head to West Memphis, Arkansas, and decide to stop at the TA Truck Stop. I turn off the interstate highway, and the street leading into the truck stop is underwater. This is a big truck; not to worry, I will just drive through it. I do drive through the water, but some of the time it was sure getting deep.

I fuel the truck so I can get a free shower. Truck stops give free shower tickets when a driver fuels his truck. One of the perks they offer for the high price of their fuel, I guess. Which, in a lot of cases, is definitely welcomed by the driver and others who are around him.

Before I shower, I decide to eat some dinner. I sit down at the counter on a stool next to the end, where the waitresses' stations are. One of the guys sitting there tells me I will need to be crazy to sit here. I responded, "Well, I should fit right in if that is the criterion for sitting here." This fellow says I can sit down anyway.

The waitress handed me a menu and asked if I could read or if I would like her to recite the good stuff. I said, "I like it when you talk dirty." Everyone laughed, and one of them said that I should fit in really well here. The driver next to me asked who I drove for and how long I have been with them. Common questions among drivers sitting in cafés. I responded that I drove for B&R out of Little Rock and that my tenure was about a month.

This statement got a strange look from one of the drivers, and he said, "Have you been with them for ten years or one month? Make up your mind." This got another big laugh from the group, and then the waitress said, "Here, you read the menu while I go recite the good stuff to Einstein over there."

The guy on the end stool and one of the waitresses are in love. Everyone at the counter knows this, for the talk is about when they are going to get married. One waitress tells the guy they should get married now, and one of the truck drivers tells her the guy must take a load to South Texas first. That way they both have a way out of this impending marriage, to which everyone laughs. I butt in and say, "I have this alter ego who is the Reverend Le Roy, and I could do the ceremony now for a modest fee."

All the guys at the counter have now joined in with the well-wishing for the happy couple. They are talking back and forth about when these lovebirds should do this dastardly deed. The driver, lovebird, says if the wedding is now, he still must take the load to Texas, and he would miss the honeymoon. All the other drivers ask to be his stand-in for this part. Everyone is laughing and having a good time. Of course, this is all a joke, and I'm not sure the happy couple even knew each other better than, "Yes, bring me a menu, and I will have a cup of coffee."

Sometimes, the conversations get a little strange, like, "Hi there, yes I would like some coffee, and would you marry me right now because I've been away from home a long time, and I think I love you."

I finish my dinner and go take a shower. Then I go back into the café for another cup of coffee. I am surprised to see the same group sitting there, except for the lucky groom. He has left for Texas. I was wearing my black cap again covering the TV Preacher hair before the shower.

Now that I am all cleaned up, I have become "Reverend Le Roy of the Church of What's Happening Now Brother." I sit down on the same stool with most of the same crowd. This is due to the bad weather, and most of these drivers are now here for the night. The same waitress brought me more coffee and then recognized me as the guy in the black cap who was going to perform the wedding ceremony. "Well, I have my preacher hair on. Where is the groom so we can get on with this wedding?" This brought about a very strange look from the waitress and much laughter from everyone else.

Chapter Nine

I have had all the fun I can stand. I decide to leave and go to Little Rock this evening and stop at Love's Country Store for the night. The next morning, I would unload the produce and then head to the office.

Before going to my two stops to unload, I called the office early in the morning. The dispatcher gave me a list of all the items which go to the second stop. He said all the rest goes to the first stop. I don't question the wisdom of this, for I don't want to confuse the guy this early in the day. If he got confused, he might screw everything up all day long. I am extremely glad, however, that the company has a man working at Affiliated Foods to unload our trucks. When he asked about the list, I just shrugged my shoulders, and he knew what I meant.

Trucking companies can take the simplest things and screw them up so bad Einstein would get a headache trying to figure them out. Murphy is alive and well in the trucking industry. Murphy was born in the trucking industry.

Monday, April 15th. It is noon, I am at the office of B&R, and we are trying to decide which of the new Kenworths I am going to drive. I need to take the Freightliner to Pac Lease for service. I will stay there since it is next to the Kenworth dealership until they decide which one of the new trucks I am to take. Decisions of this nature must not be rushed, or it gets the ownership of the trucking company in a dither. At five-thirty, they finally decide which of the six new trucks I am to be the proud driver of. It is the one the dealership has ready. Brilliant. Yes, I concur. This is a good plan if I have ever heard a good plan in my life. Yes, this is a good one. I put all my junk and dirty clothes in the new KW and get out of there before someone changes their mind.

I go to a little diesel fuel stop on I-30 and spend the night. I also arrange my belongings in the new truck. The new Kenworth is somewhat different from the Freightliner I have been driving. The KW is a T600 Aerodyne with a series 60 Detroit engine and a nine-speed overdrive transmission. The cab is narrower than the Freightliner's, but the sleeper is much larger. The sleeper compartment of the Kenworth is sixty inches long and over seven feet wide and is seven feet from the floor to the roof. It has a much nicer interior, with button-tucked vinyl everywhere. It has two beds, one over the other. The KW has one air conditioner for the cab and one for the sleeper with separate controls. The heaters are the same way. There is also a windshield and side windows in the sleeper. The KW is also about ten inches taller than the Freightliner. The series 60 engine in the KW is larger and has more horsepower.

I have always been partial to the KW over all other brands, but I will admit that the Freightliner rides very well, even though it has a spring suspension. This KW has an air ride. One of the other differences I like is the KW has electric mirrors. The KW has as many gauges as a Boeing 747; well, almost. I fold down the top bunk to sleep there so I can look out at the stars before I close my eyes for the night.

Tuesday, April 16th. I get to the office at 8:00 a.m., and I ask about a load going west. They have not decided which trailer I am to take yet. Oh no, not another day like yesterday. Oh yes, another day like yesterday. The only difference is we are talking trailers and not trucks today. They also need to get me a load that will take me to my house.

Same day, only later, much later. It is now 3:00 p.m., and I am still waiting for the decision. They have three new trailers at Thermo King being finished. They tell me one will be done today, and it will be mine. Bill, the owner of B&R, also has found me a load.

The load is chickens, dead chickens, and going to a grocery store distributing company in Los Angeles, California. Yay, team. I am going to be an Arkansas chicken hauler. Let's get them chickens on board cause we're going to the house. "When are these yard birds due to arrive in L.A.," I asked. I am presuming Monday, next. Bill tells me they deliver on Friday. I think we have a problem here because I have been gone from home a month now and I do not intend to just go by the house at seventy miles an hour and wave. I would actually want to stop and stay stopped for two or three days," I said.

You would think I was the one who thrust the dagger and thus created a mortal wound. To put this into Southern, ol' Bill was taken aback. Bill then said, "I think we have a problem here. I guess I will need to put someone else on this truck to haul the chickens."

"You do have a problem because I believe I can find an airplane that will take me to Albuquerque. You certainly are going to need to find another driver to take your chickens on to Los Angeles." I explained.

About this time, the head dispatcher, vice-president of the company, the guy who keeps Bill straight, and the self-appointed head chief in charge (Jerry told me yesterday he ran this company) came over to help out. He tells Bill this is not the plan, and he will need to find me another load going west. I am too good of a driver to run off this way.

Bill finds a load of paper going to Los Angeles within ten minutes, and the safety man tells me I should just pick one of the trailers that are parked out front on the street. We go look them over. Two of them are 1989 models and look like they are in good shape. I go back in the office to get the details of the load and one of the dispatchers asked me if I would go to

Thermo King to pick up one of the new trailers. I am so happy they have finally straightened everything out; I say fine.

I go to Thermo King, get the new trailer, and take it back to the office. Thermo King is on the other side of Little Rock, and the trip takes an hour. When I get back the trailer I was going to pull is gone. My blood pressure is now at the boiling point, but I stay calm and tell the safety man about this new problem. We cuss and discuss the way that no one in this company talks to each other and that no one knows what the other is thinking.

"Big problem, and you need to get your act together," I say. He agrees with me and says he will lose drivers if this kind of thing continues. I tell him I have threatened to quit two times now and I would not make such a threat again. The next thing that gets this fouled up from poor management and it affects me, I will just call it experience and take it to the house. He said he understood and hoped things would not be this way in the future. I also told him I knew there wasn't any effort made to get me on a load to the West Coast. He also agreed to this and explained that he had told Bill if we don't do as we agreed when we hired you that you probably would quit. "You got that right partner," I said. He then told me to get out of town with the trailer I picked up from Thermo King before someone steals the darn thing. "I'm gone," I said.

The paper is to load sometime tonight in Jonesboro, Arkansas. The reason they tell me sometime tonight is they are still running the stuff on the presses and will load me as soon as they get the magazines on pallets.

I start north in the direction of Jonesboro, and I start to reflect on my month in the southeast. I have seen some very unusual things on this trip. I start to think about going to the west coast again. When I left Little Rock for the first time to go to the southeast, I was traveling in a new country for me. I had never driven a truck in the southeastern part of the country. I have been almost everywhere else in the country but not the southeast. I know where most of the truck stops in the western part of the nation are. I know which to stop at and which ones to avoid. Maybe this is what made this trip so full of different experiences for me.

φ

I think back to some of the trips to the West Coast, and I wonder if it will be the same with this company. I drove for a company in New Mexico that did just about the same type of trucking except for the ice cream. This was the first time I had hauled ice cream. The company I worked for in the land of enchantment hauled meat out and usually produce back. Well, that is not exactly right either. They hauled meat outbound and hauled produce anywhere in the country.

I once hauled a load of produce from Yuma, Arizona, to Boston. From Boston, I went to St. Albans, Vermont, which is the land of the little people and then hauled a load of chocolate rabbits to Plainview, Texas. The rabbits were for Walmart. I'll bet you thought I was going to say for Easter. Why, of course, they were for Easter.

I think about some of the strange things I have seen in California, like the time I was going to Los Angeles from Washington with a load of apples.

About sixty miles north of Sacramento, there is a truck stop called "Panty Hose Junction." I stopped there for dinner that night and after I got my glass of iced tea, I overheard a strange conversation.

These guys were sitting across from my booth. They sounded, from what I heard, like they were planning to kill someone. That got my attention. One guy tells the other, "I should have shot the S.O.B. If I could have reached my gun, I would have for sure." The other one then said if he had seen him quicker, he would have run him off the road, even if it meant smashing up his new truck. Anybody who would do a thing like that should be shot, he continued. The other one agreed and said just shooting the guy wasn't enough; he should also be hung by a rusty chain and then dragged into Nevada, over all the cactus in the State.

Now I think to myself whatever this guy has done must be very bad. In fact, I'm not sure what anyone could have done to warrant this type of punishment. He must have killed a lot of people or something.

By nature, I think I am somewhat curious, but now these guys go back to their eating and say no more. Well, it gets the best of me, and I can't stand it anymore. I have got to find out what these guys are, or were, talking about.

It is sort of like this old cowboy friend of mine from Oklahoma City who always said, if you don't tell me, I will lasso yah and drag yah through the cow pies until yah talks.

Well, I wasn't going to resort to that, but I was bound and determined to ask, real nice. "Who are you guys planning to kill," I asked. They both grinned and started to tell me the story.

Well, as I have already said, I must have easy listening stamped on my forehead. Because of what they told me, I just about couldn't hardly believe-it.

Hell, and I'm from Texas, the land of the tall tales. The place where bull crap grows on trees and hides almost everywhere. The stuff is just waiting to jump on the poor, unsuspecting listener. I have even known Bud Hendigart, one of the last of the cowboy freaks, and listened to some of his yarns, but they didn't match this one.

I'll bet not many people even know what a cowboy freak is. Well, he is a feller from the Texas Panhandle who was born a hundred years too late. For the way he talks and acts is just about how Festus was in Gunsmoke. Bud wore a cowboy hat that had two or three hypodermic needles, just the needles stuck in the top. Now he was not a junkie; he had never met one. The needles were for giving a steer a shot if it were sick. He kept the needles there so they wouldn't get bent. Ol Bud's idea of a junkie would be a pickup truck with a busted fender.

These fellows tell me that yesterday, they were in Los Angeles and were headed for Ontario on I-60. They work for the same trucking company, had loaded at the same place, and were now taking their loads to Portland. They were driving in the center lane when a little blue Mazda RX 7 pulled alongside the truck that was in the rear of their little convoy and just stayed right beside him until the driver looked down into the car. The man in the car was fat, and from what they could see of his head, he was about fifty years old. The man did not have on one stitch of clothes, I mean stark naked, except for this little ribbon tied, well, you know where. As soon as the driver looked at him, he sped up to the first truck and did the same thing. After the lead driver had seen him, he stepped on the gas and, in no time, turned off the highway and was gone.

After they told me this tale, they started again with the "I should have shot him, the dirty S.O.B." "Well guys, thanks for the info; if I ever see him, I will shoot him for you," I said.

They paid for their dinners and went on down the road. I sat there eating my dinner and thinking about the story they had told me. I bet those two guys have more fun telling that crazy story. I envision them coming into a truck stop and telling it to anyone they think will listen to their wild tales. I thought it might be a story to remember, but by the next day, I had all but forgotten it.

81

I spent the night at a roadside park and, the next morning went into Los Angeles. I found the produce market, which is near the downtown area. Once loaded and driving to the drop-off place, I found out that I couldn't unload 'til late that evening. In fact, they told me I couldn't unload 'til in the morning. Well, I'm here and finally got the truck empty at five a.m. I slept for four hours before heading to Ontario to the truck stop there.

About ten a.m. I was driving east on Highway 60, and guess what pulls alongside my truck. You got it, the blue Mazda RX only today he had on a red ribbon. I was laughing so hard that if I had a desire to run him over, I probably would have missed him. I wondered where the California Highway Patrol was when you need them. They always seem to be where you don't want them to be and never around at the right time.

φ

Back to the present, I head in the direction of Jonesboro and get there about nine in the evening. I get backed into the dock, and the shipper tells me they have only two of the twenty pallets ready to load. I tell him I am going to unhook and go into town to eat dinner.

I go to a very nice Mexican food restaurant and have a wonderful repast. I am using that word again. The waiter and I have some very stimulating conversations after I order in Spanish. Does it surprise you that I can do that? Especially after how I talked ugly about New Mexico. Well, I speak four languages: Texan, English, Profane, and Spanish. Now that I am flatulent from the Burrito, I shall repair to my conveyance and go check on the progress of the loading. I always try to keep 'em guessing about me.

I get back to the publishing company, hook up to the trailer again, and go inside. It is now eleven in the evening, and the shift at this plant is about to change. One of the shippers from the current shift asked me what load I was picking up. I tell him it is the one for Los Angeles, California. He goes up to the front of the building to check on the progress of the printing because he does not have the paperwork for the load in the shipping office.

Is Murphy about to strike again? We shall see, for here comes the shipping clerk now.

Chapter Ten

The shipper tells me that according to the press schedule they will not even start on this magazine until tomorrow. I tell him one of the other guys said they already had two pallets ready to load. He tells me that's right, but the broker said to run the one going to the East Coast first because there was no hurry on the West Coast load. It doesn't deliver until Monday afternoon of next week. "You mean they sent this truck here to pick up this load and it is not even printed yet?" I said. The guy tells me this is very common to have a truck sit here for two days.

"When will this be ready to load?" I asked. "I'm afraid not until very late tomorrow night and more than likely not until the next day," he explained.

"You are sure about this because if this is true, I won't be here to haul it," I said.

"Oh, it's true enough, all right," he said. "Have a nice night," I said as I went out the door.

I stopped at the payphone in the hall. I called my wife Diana and told her I would call her tomorrow and tell her what time my plane would land in Albuquerque.

"Short-lived stay driving the new Aerodyne Kenworth," I thought as I walked in the direction of the truck. I climbed into the cab, started the engine, and headed in the direction of Little Rock, Arkansas.

"To the nearest airport," I shout. With great glee and with the gusto of a hound dog, I break wind from this place. Remember I had dined at a Mexican restaurant. I grab for the little bottle containing the Maalox and chew on a couple of the ill-tasting tablets. *"This truck driving could kill a person,"* I thought as I shifted into high gear and wound the big Detroit engine up. I think I made record time from Jonesboro to Little Rock that evening. I think I averaged seventy-eight miles an hour the entire way.

Wednesday morning, April 17th. I am at the airport anxiously awaiting departure on the first flight to Albuquerque, America. I deposited the Kenworth at the dealership because it was close to the airport. This is after my explanation to the powers that be at B&R. We had a considerable amount of discussion on the reasons that brought me back to Little Rock. He couldn't believe I would not wait for days to get the load. I told him I could not believe he would ask me to wait for days to be loaded. I could see we weren't getting anywhere with this discussion so I told him to have a nice life and send my check in the mail.

Now, I sit in anxious anticipation and odious vapor, awaiting the arrival of the aforementioned airplane. I hope the air-conditioning is working on this airplane because I might be offensive to my neighbors. The reason for this is that with all the screwing around, I have been unable to properly bathe for the last two days. Stink as I may, I shall just have to offend, for I shall be on that airplane only barring the impending coming of the Lord before 12:20 p.m. today. I shall properly bathe and disinfect upon arrival home unless this aforementioned phenomenon occurs, which would necessitate standing before God in a slightly soiled manner. Yeah, the appointed time of departure approaches, and I am gladdened to the cockles of my heart.

I am doing this writing in the coffee shop at the airport, and the one thought I am having as I look around me is, "Everyone sure looks clean."

I think back on my stay in the wilds of Florida. I had occasion to study the social and cultural habits of a tribe of people who inhabit the interior regions of that state. This tribe is sometimes referred to as the migratory "New Yorker." Some of the more affluent of this tribe also inhabit the exterior regions of Florida. I have seen their boats docked just about everywhere. I even saw one parked in the parking lot of a McDonalds. Lowering the motor on these boats in a parking lot does irreparable damage to the craft's propeller. I saw this happen on one occasion in Florida City. Florida City is just south of the tribal headquarters known as Miami.

The appointed time for departure is at hand, and I shall have a ceremonial drinking of the concoction known as a Bloody Mary. This magic elixir greatly enhances flying and keeps one from caring about certain noxious odors.

We have departed Little Rock, and I am in one of the seats that face each other on Southwest Airlines. I am surrounded by four ladies who work for Mid Con, whatever that is. I hope these ladies all suffer from sinus trouble. Not so, for one of the ladies is getting up to change seats.

The other three are discussing a common topic among young mothers nowadays. The wearing of clothing adorned with Ninja Turtles which seems to be a rage among the preschool generation.

We are above the clouds now and clipping right along. I need to be home, for my concentration is fading, and my mind is wandering in the direction of my impending bath. If it can be truly said that some people's minds are in the toilet, I can say I am suffering from this affliction. I am becoming extremely self-conscious about this condition, which I find myself in. I know I must be curling the hair in the proboscis of these ladies.

I am now in Dallas, and in two hours, I will be home. I feel like E. T., for the one word I hear in my mind right now is "HOME." I shall rejoice and make merry, kill the fatted calf, and take a shower. These things will not occur in the order written; I can assure you. The shower will take precedence over everything except the welcoming hugs and kisses from my lovely wife. Once the bathing is completed the making merry and the killing of the fatted calf shall begin.

I have noticed the ugly factor has had a forty or fifty percent increase in this leg of the journey to Albuquerque. Some of the people are downright ugly, and their mothers dress them funny. I saw that saying on a cap in Georgia. I should have bought it. There is a woman dressed in the same type of outfit, with a hat, that the woman from Santa Fe wore on TV when she was flying to Iraq to retrieve her spouse. I don't think Paris is ready for this "Santa Fe Style." It is in the land of enchantment, known as K-Mart's upper middle class.

From the way the sky is looking I should be glad I have taken an early plane. Dallas may think they have had enough rain lately, but I believe it is not finished yet. The gods of rain may present themselves in full force tonight.

It is now 1:45 p.m. Mountain Time, and we have taken off from Dallas, and I have reset my watch. I am now dining on peanuts and a coke and this repast should keep me from getting malnutrition before I get home. They are giving out pretzels. Wow, this must be the dinner flight! I have this craving to try to consume a large supreme pizza all by myself. I will refuse to eat anything this evening that comes wrapped in plastic or can be purchased from a vending machine in a truck stop. I realize that totally eliminates one of the basic food groups from my diet this evening. The snack food group, which has the scientific name "junk," will not touch my lips tonight. Munching on a large pizza sounds very good right about now.

We must still be over Texas because the land below is either in squares or circles. If we were in New Mexico, the land would be undefined and run in all directions. Navigation is more difficult when there are no squares and circles to go by.

Chapter Eleven

My mind is in reverse gear now and I am thinking about some of the other adventures I have had while driving a truck. Alas, I have been remiss in not mentioning my part-time co-driver. Even though he didn't accompany me on this adventure, he has done so many times in the past. This part-time companion is a very unique fellow and I will tell you some of the things he has done. His name is Le Roy Ras'on. The Reverend Le Roy Ras'on the last name is pronounced "rays on."

Le Roy has traveled somewhere about fifty thousand miles in the truck with me. In October 1989, after I had given up on becoming another Leonardo Di Vinci, I answered "help wanted" ads in the local newspaper from companies looking for a truck driver. I answered three ads altogether, but the first two were from large national companies who said I needed two years' recent over-the-road experience before they would hire me. The third one was a local trucking company here in New Mexico. They also wanted the two years' recent experience, and I asked the director of safety if they gave road tests to anyone they wanted to hire. I haven't even been in a truck in ten years, but I was not going to let that get in my way. He said yes, they did, to which I said: "Why not give me the road test, and you will find out whether I have forgotten how to drive the big trucks or not." He agreed to the test and told me what time to come into the office the next morning.

At 10:00 a.m. the next morning, I was ready for my turn to take this test. The truck was a 1987 Peterbilt Conventional with a four hundred-horsepower Cummins engine in it. It had a fifteen-speed Road Ranger transmission, which I had never driven.

When the first guy got back from his test, he told the rest of us they had disconnected the tachometer just to make it more interesting. Not to worry, it is just like riding a bicycle; once you know how, it is easy to get back on one. Especially when I had considered myself to be quite proficient at this sort of thing, if it has wheels and a steering wheel, I can drive it. The trailer which was used for the test was a forty-eight-footer, with the wheels all the way to the back. Still, no problem, for I once pulled a cattle trailer that was fifty-three feet long.

It was now my turn. I went through a reasonably good pre-trip inspection, even though I was certain the equipment would be okay because I had watched the other guy do the very same thing not thirty minutes ago. We climbed into the cab, and the man in the passenger seat introduced himself as Bill. Bill told me we would leave the yard and go down the access road to the first stoplight, then go north on the interstate highway for about ten miles. At the exit at the appointed spot of ten miles, I was to turn around, and he would tell me where to go from there.

I started the engine and let the oil pressure come up to sixty pounds. I carefully checked all the other gauges before I pushed in the two parking brake handles on the dash. As I sat down in the air ride seat, I noticed the shifting pattern sticker was in the lower right-hand corner of the windshield. I took my time adjusting the seat so I could study the shift pattern. It was just like an old ten-speed road ranger I had driven many times way back in the sixties. The gear shift had an extra lever on the left side and I figured that was where the extra five gears were hiding. This is going to be easier than I had expected.

I put the big truck into second gear and slowly disengaged the clutch. The Peterbilt started to roll, and I looked over at ol' Bill and said, "Which gate would you like me to exit from." I figured this would be a clever way to make him think I was very confident in what I was about to do. I shifted the truck into the next gear without using the clutch, and it went into the gear very smoothly as I turned the corner and got the big rig onto the street. Before we got to the end of the block, I have shifted again, also very smooth. I am starting to impress myself as we enter traffic on the interstate highway, and I shift to the higher gears.

I figured I would be rusty but so far, I had been smoother than goat cheese on a greased cookie sheet.

Ol' Bill tells me on the way back to come off the interstate and pretend it was a mountain and to slow the truck without using the brakes. No problem, I think, as I reach over and flip on the Jake brake and downshift two gears. A Jake brake is a device on the engine that will slow a truck down. It is used mostly on hills or going into small towns by some irreverent cowboy truck drivers. It is said this kind of guy is a retard using his retarder.

Bill looks impressed again as we head for a very narrow street that I must negotiate a right-hand turn onto. I get the truck back into the yard and back it into the appropriate parking space, which is between two other trailers. I feel very good the test is over, but I think I have done very well.

We walk to the office, and Bill goes into the safety director's office. I was standing just outside the door and could hear Bill tell the safety director, "You can send this guy anywhere in the United States today."

The safety director calls me into his office, and Bill heads out to the yard toward his next victim. As he opened the door, I thanked him and waved.

I sat in front of the safety man's desk, and he tells me to go to their doctor's office and get my medical card. He calls their office and makes the appointment for an hour from now. He then tells me as soon as I get back, they will go over all the paperwork and get me started.

I got back to the trucking company's office at 1:30 p.m., and we went through all the necessary papers by 3:30 p.m. I left for Texas the same evening at 5:30 to pick up a load of boxed meat from a slaughterhouse in Amarillo.

I went back and forth to the meat houses three times that week. On the fourth trip, they sent me to Los Angeles, California, with a load of chicken burritos. From Los Angeles, I went up the valley in California to get a load of produce.

The second stop was north of Oxnard. It was five in the evening when I was backing up to the dock to get lemons. Just as my trailer bumped the dock, the fellow who was standing on the dock watching me back up started jumping around like a frog. I got out of the truck and asked why he was jumping around like that. He said, "Didn't you feel it?" I told him, yes, I did, but I didn't hit the dock hard enough to cause that kind of jumping around.

"NO, didn't you feel the dock shake?" he asked. "No, I didn't hit it that hard," I repeated. "It felt like an earthquake," he exclaimed. "No, I didn't hit the dock that hard," I said with a slightly puzzled look. "I don't mean you hit the dock that hard. I mean, it felt like a real earthquake," he said. "No, I didn't feel a thing. This truck has air ride, and it shakes a little while I am backing into the dock," I responded.

We started putting the lemons on the truck, and the dock man brought out a little portable TV and turned it on the channel to get the World Series. We stopped loading when the news flash came on that San Francisco and Oakland were just hit by a big earthquake just before the start of the World Series baseball game.

Now loaded with lemons, I left Oxnard and headed in the direction of Bakersfield to pick up some carrots. I thought if there was a really big earthquake, I should call my wife and tell her I am okay. I go to where the truckers call the "shaky side" of the USA, and the darn thing tries to fall off into the ocean. If my wife has heard this on the television, she will think I am in the big middle of it.

I stop and call her to let her know I was all right and that from where I was I didn't even feel the quake. She had seen the televised reports of the quake and was worried. Especially when she saw a white semi dangling off of the Oakland Bay Bridge going into San Francisco. She wasn't sure where I was exactly in California but sure was glad to hear from me and that I was okay.

I got all the veggies loaded the next day and took off for Salt Lake City. I load with canned green beans in Salt Lake and head back to Albuquerque.

In four trips I have been in four different trucks. I was getting tired of putting all my stuff in a truck and then taking it out again in a few days. If I was going to be a trucker, I wanted a truck. I wanted a truck to be assigned to me so I could leave my things in it all the time. I found out this idea was a good one, but it originally didn't work out as I had envisioned. Every time I wanted a day off to stay at the house, they would send my truck out with another driver on it. They could have sent the truck to one of the meat houses in Texas, and the truck would have been back the next day. I would have had a day off, and everyone would be happy. Well, it didn't work out that way. Inevitably, they would send my truck to New York City or someplace just as far, and it would be a week and a half before I would see it again.

I asked for and received a truck of my very own. It was a new Kenworth T600, silver with blue stripes. The T600 is commonly referred to as the anteater because of the way the hood slopes down from the windshield. I personally think it should be called a Roman nose, after a horse I once had.

I decided that Le Roy should accompany me on the truck, and with a little persuasion, he did. I took many pictures of Le Roy in various parts of the United States over the next four months. One of the pictures was taken at the Continental Divide on top of Wolf Creek Pass in Southern Colorado.

I had taken a load of food to a store in Farmington, New Mexico, and was told by the dispatcher to go to Alamosa, Colorado, and get a load of potatoes. Just as I was leaving Farmington at about 11:00 p.m., it started to snow. By the time I had gone twelve miles to the town of Aztec, there were inches of the white stuff on the road. I decided to try to go on to Alamosa if the snow didn't get so bad that I couldn't make it. I got about twenty miles north of Aztec to where there is a rather steep hill, and here is where I told Le Roy we should go back to Aztec before we got into deep trouble. The snow there was six to eight inches deep, and it was still snowing very hard. We went back to the safety of civilization for the rest of the night.

When I got up the next morning, the snow was six inches deep in Aztec. I had breakfast, and we took off toward Durango, Colorado. The same hill where I had chickened out the night before was still there and had more snow than it did then. About ten trucks were sitting on the side of the road, working up their courage and putting on chains. I decided this was an appropriate way to attack the hill and put my chains on. I chained three of the rear-drive tires and one of the trailer tires. I did this because I was empty, and I didn't want the trailer to try to pass me going down a hill.

I was the first brave soul to attempt the hill, and I got over the top without a problem. There were a couple of cars that were not as fortunate, for they were stuck in the snow. I got to the steep downhill just before you reach Highway 160 and got a real thrill. I was very glad I had put the chains on the trailer because, going down the hill, the trailer tried to pass me once. I knew the rest of the day was going to be fun because compared to Wolf Creek Pass, what I had just completed was nothing. To make a fair comparison, it would be like a pimple on an elephant's butt.

I have a sticker on my briefcase that reads "No Guts, No Glory." I think that was the slogan for the Kamikaze pilots in WWII. Well, I have another saying that has got me into trouble in the past, and I think I said it to Le Roy that morning. I looked at him and said. "Well, Columbus took a chance." I think Le Roy's face turned a shade of purple.

We made it to the top of the pass and I took some pictures of Le Roy sitting on a three-foot snowbank with the sign that says "Wolf Creek Pass." In the winter, it should read, "You have made it to the Top; now, what are you going to do." As I am still alive to write this, you should figure out we also made it down the other side.

One of the first trips I made to California was to Alameda Island, which is next to Oakland. This was about a week after the earthquake during the World Series. I had unloaded a trailer full of high-priced steaks in El Paso, Texas, and when I called the dispatcher, I was told to go to Hobbs, New Mexico. I proceeded to Hobbs, and when I called in, I was told to take a load of meat to the Navy Ship Yard in Alameda, California.

I got all but one pallet of the frozen meat on the truck when I was told the last pallet was not cold enough for the federal inspector. I sat around that afternoon and waited for the meat to cool. At 5:30 p.m. I was told the meat still did not meet their requirements, and I would have to wait until the morning for the last pallet to be loaded.

Hobbs doesn't have a truck stop. I had to get a motel room for the night so I could take a shower. I sat around, watched TV, and got a good night's sleep. The next morning, I went back to the meat house and loaded the last pallet of now well-frozen hamburger.

I took off for California and had a nice drive until I arrived in Bakersfield. Just before getting into town, I had asked a driver which was the best way to get from Highway 99 to Interstate 5. I was told to take the Oil Dale exit on the north side of Bakersfield. Then, when I get on the off-ramp, I was told to go to the stop sign and then turn left. That highway would take me over to the interstate highway, and it was a good road.

I found the exit, which said Oil Dale, and stopped at the sign at the bottom of the off-ramp. There were two roads to the left. The one to the left didn't look as good as the right-left one did. I took the right left. Murphy was about to show me how he worked in the trucking business. Murphy was about to kick my butt.

φ

Now, I should explain I have an uncanny sense of direction. I don't get lost very easily and then I usually know where I am, or at least how to get to where I'm not lost anymore. I had a cousin and his wife with me one night in my bass boat on Lake Texoma. We had been fishing under the Washington Bridge and decided to go back across the lake to where we had set some jug lines in a cove. During the time we were fishing it had gotten dark, very dark, and it was about seven miles back to the cove. My cousin's wife asked me how we were going to find the right cove in the dark. No problem, I told her. I can find it in the dark, for I have a great sense of direction. We drove across the lake at about forty miles per hour with only the running lights on. When I stopped to shine my spotlight around, we were only fifty feet from the jug lines. She was impressed, to say the least. So was I.

φ

I didn't look at the map which still wouldn't have told me two roads were leading left from the off-ramp. I just decided the road I needed to take was the best-looking of the two. I went a few miles down this road and went through the little town of Oil Dale. A couple of miles further down the road, I came to some oil fields. I had watched a movie with Chris Kristofferson in it that was shot in Oil Dale. I was thinking about the movie and not whether this was the road I should be on. I went a few miles further, and I thought, if this is the right road, California sure has some wild-looking hills. I had not been in this part of the state before. I had no way of knowing whether I had taken the correct "left" road, but if I had, I would have been in farming country and flat land.

All signs of civilization departed, not even a single car coming down the road. The hill was getting steeper and steeper by the mile. By the time I realized I had screwed up, I couldn't turn the truck around.

The road became narrower and steeper, and I was loaded very heavy. I was down into first gear and running out of power. I was also beginning to sweat even though it was overcast and cool that afternoon. And Le Roy was really turning purple now and hanging on for dear life. I found out where the lower five gears were on this truck.

Now, I might point out that even if you are loaded heavy, this truck, and most trucks like it, start off from a stop in second gear. If there is a little incline you might need to use first gear to start off with. On a big hill, I have never had to go below first gear to get up it. I have never had to use the lower five gears at all, never. Until now.

I went from fifth under, down to fourth, then third, then second. The road became so steep and narrow I was starting to think about saying my prayers. On one curve my left front tire was no more than five inches from God, a drop off of about three hundred feet, and my right-side trailer tires were rubbing against the rocks which were next to the road on that side.

The hills were steep, and nothing was growing over one foot high, just grass. Not a tree in sight, and I still didn't have any idea where the top of this thing was. I just knew if it were any steeper, I was in a heap of trouble because I only had one gear left. I was already down to about three miles per hour. To stop would have been a suicide at this point.

The only living things I saw were some cows that must have had on traction master shoes to stand on the sides of those hills. One wrong step, and they would have become hamburger on the hoof. Some little ground squirrels stood on rocks at the side of the road to watch me lumber past them. I know I saw at least one of these squirrels laughing as I went by, and if I could have stopped, I would have thrown a rock at him for making fun of me. But I think he knew I had screwed up and was laughing because he had never seen a truck of this size before on this road.

The road flattened out a bit, and I got all the way into the regular first gear. I even had a chance to wipe the beads of sweat from my forehead. I made the next corner and saw the tops of some trees about a quarter of a mile in front of me. A little further down the road, I saw a house with a driveway that was big enough for me to get the truck into. After backing into the driveway, I just sat there for a minute, thinking about how I had fouled up and if I could get the truck back down that road.

It is easier to go up than down, especially when it is that steep. I knew I couldn't go any further up this road because I felt I had already used up all the good luck I was going to find today. I had spent just over two hours going twenty-four miles. The first twelve miles of it was at fifty miles per hour.

I heard a sound to my left and saw a little Honda motorbike coming into the driveway. I got out of the truck in a hurry and waved to the old man on the cycle. He rode over to where I was standing and turned the engine off.

"Hi, how are you doing?" I asked. "A lot better than you if you came up that way," he said, pointing in the direction I had just come from. "I have lived here thirty-two years and I don't think I have ever seen a truck that big ever come up that road. I have seen some bobtail cattle trucks and some small highway department trucks, but never anything that big, no sir I haven't."

Now, I felt a hell of a lot better, knowing I had just done something nobody else had ever done. Not counting the fact that I could have lost a seventy-thousand-dollar truck, a thirty-thousand-dollar trailer, and no telling how much money's worth of Navy meat. Not to mention, my own little body could have been smashed to bits. Yep, I feel just proud as punch for this feat of driving skill I have just accomplished.

"Is there any way I can get the hell off this hill without going back the way I came?" I asked the old man. "If this road gets any worse, I am not sure I can go much further," I added.

"Oh, no problem," said the old man, "you can go about a hundred more yards down the road, and you will come to a stop sign. Now, don't turn right because the road will get worse that way. You will want to go left if you are headed to Highway 99, and you can drive fifty miles an hour if you want to."

I turned left and made it back to the highway and then found a road that crossed the farmland in the valley. I breathed a sigh of relief when I saw Interstate 5 coming up in front of me. I have seen the town of Woody, California, and I have lived to tell about it, and I have no desire to ever see that place again.

I didn't take any pictures of Le Roy on that excursion. I was too busy and he was hanging on for dear life. I know he shriveled up a bit and didn't want his picture taken because of the new wrinkles.

Road Express still has a copy of the picture with Le Roy on Wolf Creek Pass in their dispatch office. I also took pictures of Le Roy with a Saguaro cactus in southern Arizona and one with a Joshua Tree in the Mohave Desert in California. There is one picture overlooking the Columbia River in Washington.

Le Roy has done a lot more than just sit in the truck and pose for pictures. He also has had a lot of fun waving at the girls passing by. He also has been in on a few very funny instances.

I was going south on California 101 after leaving San Francisco in mid-November 1989 when this Red Peterbilt passed me. The guy in the Peterbilt says on his CB, "Your co-driver sure looks funny sitting there." I told him his name was Le Roy and asked what was so funny about him. He said, "The guy looks a little weird, don't you think?" I then asked him what was weird about a guy with a purple face. Well, from the sound of shock in his voice, I wasn't sure what he thought. He said, "You guys must be very good friends for you to call a black man purple."

I guess he needs to get a better look at Le Roy, so I step on the gas and pass the Peterbilt. What that driver said next, I could not understand because of the laughter. We had to go into one of those weigh stations California is famous for, and we didn't get to finish the conversation. I sometimes wonder what that guy told his wife if he has one, about meeting Le Roy.

I bet he is more careful with his word association from now on. We often identify people and things by the names we have put on them. Some people, and I don't think they are all bigots, will associate a name with something they perceive it to be. This is a problem we as humans often have in that everything is not always as we perceive it to be.

I, unfortunately, have had this perception problem from time to time. I have had a very hard time believing a hamburger could have square meat. I, ever since I was a little tyke, have had the belief a hamburger was round meat. If I ever tried one of the square ones, I might find they are good. So far, I have resisted the temptation to eat one.

φ

That reminds me of the time in Oklahoma when I was having a new home built. I had bought five acres east of Norman and had a contractor hired to do the building of my new house. The plans called for the second-story plumbing to be located on an outside wall. I had a very close friend who was working toward his Doctorate in Architecture at the University of Oklahoma. This friend wanted to look at my house plans, and discovered the error, and reworked them to put the plumbing on an inside wall where they belonged.

Have I mentioned this friend was black? Well, so was his entire family, his wife, and his three children. I might also mention they were from Ghana, West Africa. Ed has a very distinct British accent. His wife Rosena had not mastered American southern English either. Her accent was so profound it made her difficult to understand sometimes.

One day, while the building was going on at the house, Ed and his family drove out to check on the progress and also for a visit. I was behind the house with the construction crew, who were setting the septic tank when Ed came walking through the trees. One of the construction crew said, "Look, here comes a negra." Ed walked up to me and said in the Queen's English, "Oh, I say, Tom, they have made a good bit of progress since we were here last."

About this time, Rosena motioned for Ed to come see what his children were looking at. Ed smiled and told me he would be right back, and turned and walked to where his family and my wife were standing. The construction crew all had a very surprised look on their faces. The one who had made the racial remark said, "I can't believe I just called that fellow a "Negra." Then he started to apologize for what he had said. I told him "I don't think I am the one that needs the apology."

I know what human nature is, and it is not always what we would like it to be. If we would not be so quick to judge or classify someone by the color of their skin or their religion, we might be better off as the human race. It sounds great, and I wish it were true that we all tried to behave a little better toward our fellow man. We would be on a higher plane of humanity than we are now.

Alas, I have lapsed into another period of Philosophy. I don't classify my Philosophical views in the same order as Plato, Socrates, or Joan Rivers.

Chapter Twelve

I left Los Angeles with a load of Quaker State oil in barrels and headed for Kent, Washington. This would be new territory for me. I have trucked all over the state of California but not into Oregon or Washington. I head north on Interstate 5 and am looking forward to the new sights I would see. I was talking on the CB to a fellow from Medford, Oregon, and it was about eight in the evening. We talked on as we passed Sacramento, and this fellow asked me if I had ever been to "Panty Hose Junction." He tells me it has a good café and he would like to stop and eat dinner and wants to know if I want to stop with him. We stop, and the café was as he told me, a good café. The name comes from the waitresses wearing short skirts and black lace hose. Most truck stops don't have sights to see that rivals the quality of the food. This one does and may be the reason the place does a very good business. Their parking lot was full, and we had to park in an overflow area, which was dirt.

I spent the night just north of Redding and, the next morning, went to Medford, Oregon. I have two cousins who live there, and I have not seen them in over twenty years. We have a good visit for five hours, and then I head north again toward Kent, Washington.

The scenery is very good since leaving Redding. The mountains of northern California are very pretty, and Mount Shasta is quite spectacular. The Siskiyou Summit is a real hill that gives the trucker a thrill going down. Any hill that has two runaway ramps is a challenge, even in good weather. Those who go down it often may think it is not bad, but if it is not, why do they have the two runaway ramps? An old and wise trucker once told me a very profound thing about mountain passes. He said, "You can go down a thousand hills too slow but only one too fast." Being a flatlander myself, I have taken those words of wisdom to heart and am very careful on seven percent grades when the truck has a gross weight of close to eighty thousand pounds.

The three little passes north of Rogue River, Oregon, are not much of a threat unless the weather is bad with fog and snow. The valleys going north on Interstate 5 are very green, with pine-covered hills and valleys with lush grass. In the early mornings of November, these valleys are shrouded in mist and fog. I took many pictures of these beautiful sights.

I head into Portland, Oregon, and cross the Columbia River. It is very spectacular, to say the least. The Columbia and the Willamette Rivers sure do beat Horse Creek of the Texas Panhandle in the amount of water they have in them. Of course, they do because Horse Creek is dry most of the time. I think they were going to damn up Horse Creek until they figured out it would take fifteen years to get enough water to make a lake.

I find the exit the man from the Quaker State warehouse had given me as part of the instructions to find their location. After about two hours of driving around in some of the most gosh-awful places I have ever taken a truck, I find the appointed place to unload the oil. The exit he gave me was four miles from the one I should have turned on. Some of the roads I was on that morning were not fit for a mountain goat, let alone a semi-truck. After I got the oil into their warehouse, I ask about who had given me the directions, and it was the forklift driver. I told the manager that in the future this guy should not be allowed to do anything except drive the forklift in an area that he is very familiar with. I also asked the manager if this guy has had any trouble finding his way to work in the mornings. For his next birthday, you should buy him a road map of the area and point out the location of your warehouse to him.

I go to a roadside park and call in from a payphone. The dispatcher tells me to go to Queens Valley, Oregon, and pick up a load of Christmas Trees. I look the place up on the map and find it is southwest of Portland, about sixty miles. I get the directions to the place and drive there in about five hours.

It is almost dark when I finally get to a sign on the side of the road that says Queens Valley Tree Farm. I turn right and follow the dirt road up a hill, and the further I go, the narrower the road gets. I look over at Le Roy and say," If this road gets any narrower, you will need to sit behind me."

The road goes around a sharp curve and ends about fifty yards past a house on the right. I think I have gone up a creek and find I have no paddle. I back down the road to the house and stop. It is dark now, and I mean dark, on this side of the hill. It must be a mile and a half to the pavement, and backing down this hill in the dark could be an all-night job.

There is a light on in the house, and I think I will see if anybody is home. I knock on the door, and a boy about twelve years old opens it. I ask him where the heck I am and where is the Queens Valley Tree Farm. He smiles and tells me that I was as lost as the last trucker who was here an hour ago. He told me the truck looked just like the one I was driving. I ask the boy how he got out of there.

The boy told me this guy backed all the way to the pavement. I told him it was daylight then, and with light, it could be done fairly easily with a good driver. Remembering how steep and curvy the road was, I thought it might be better to try to turn the truck around if I could. I ask the boy if he would help me back into their driveway so I could turn the truck around. We had to take down an old fence next to the driveway and I finally got the trailer into the yard far enough to make the turn.

Once I got the thing headed in the right direction, I got out, gave the lad a five-dollar bill, and thanked him for his help. He must have thanked me ten times before I got back into the truck. From the looks of the house and the surroundings, he was very glad to have received the five dollars.

He also told me the Queens Valley Tree Farm Road was a hundred yards further down the pavement. I wonder if it would do any good to mention to the owners of the tree farm that they should move their sign to the entrance of their farm, not on the road that I, as well as others, have taken today. I find out the next morning from the way the tree farm is run that the sign misplacement is a minor indiscretion.

The next morning, there are three trucks from Road Express here to load Christmas Trees. Trees are brought into the loading yard by helicopter and there are about thirty dark-complexioned people sorting and doing the loading. These people still are wearing their shirts which are wet from crossing a certain river in Texas. I told the foreman he better hope nobody shows up in a light green car or van because he would see all his helpers disappear into the forest. I will bet there was not a green card in the bunch.

One of the girls, of which there were four and, from their looks, were sisters, told me she would count the trees as they were put on my trailer. She would make sure I got the right amount. One of the girls went to each of the trucks and did the same thing.

When we got to the grocery stores all the trucks were short, anywhere from ten to twenty-five trees each. If it were an odd number, like seven or eight each, no one would have suspected a thing. My truck was short by twenty trees, one was fifteen, and one was twenty-five short in the tree count. I now know how this tree farm was so profitable.

Back to how I got to the grocery stores to find out about the thievery that had taken place at the tree farm. I have my trees and start toward New Mexico. I go through Portland and turn onto Interstate 84 East. This highway goes along the Columbia River almost to Pendleton, Oregon. In Pendleton, I stopped for some coffee at a little café which was next to a small dirt lot truck stop. I called my wife and told her I was on my way home and I would be there in two days. I got up to pay for the coffee, and the lady behind the counter asked me if I had ever tried any of their pies, as they are homemade.

I ask, "What kind do you have." She said, "It's what kind we don't have that would be easier to tell you." "I haven't had fresh peach in a long time. Do you have that?" Oh, the pie was good, and I will remember this place. One should always remember the places that have good "anything" out here on the road.

Well, I am full of pie and coffee, and I should be able to go a long way before I stop again. I pull out onto the big road—interstate highway—and ask the first trucker I see, "Are there any hills between here and Boise, Idaho?" The guy comes back with, "Just one." "Where is it?" I ask. The fellow then said it was right in front of me, and I would start up it in about a mile. "What's it called?" I replied. "Cabbage," was his answer.

Since I have never been on this road before, I thought it would be wise to ask about the hills. I know from experience that some of the hills in the western part of the country can be rather nasty, especially in the winter. But tonight, the stars are shining, and it hasn't been very cold yet, so it should be smooth sailing from here to New Mexico.

I start up the hill. Before I go a mile, I hit the worst fog I have seen in a long time. The fog was so thick I could not see but one stripe on the highway. The hill was getting steep, for I was downshifting gears in a hurry. I am down to twenty-five miles per hour, and I can't see a thing, and the darn fog is starting to freeze on my windshield. I turn on the defrosters full blast and hit the mirror heat switch on the dash. My palms are also starting to sweat a little. I have no idea how high this hill is or how steep. I am not sure if it even has a top in this fog. I hear on the CB that the fog lifts some at the roadside park, wherever that is. There could be an elephant in the other lane, and I couldn't see him the way it is now. I have thoughts of being here until spring and then somebody finding my skinny little body up here browsing on a pinecone or a squirrel.

I get to the top of the hill, and the road flattens out a bit, and the fog lifts right on cue, for there is the roadside park. Maybe I will get off of here alive and before spring after all.

Yep, I survived Cabbage and delivered the trees in Albuquerque, where the shortages were found. But the good news is I am home for a couple of days.

It was Christmas Eve 1989, and my wife Diana, who worked for the Department of Labor in Albuquerque, had four days off for Christmas. I was scheduled to take a load of meat to Bakersfield, California, that night for delivery in the morning. I asked Diana if she wanted to come with me to California. We could spend some time roaming around Los Angeles and other such places, and she could fly back to Albuquerque on December 27th. Well, after a small amount of thought about this adventure, because she had not ever gone with me in the big trucks, she said this would be fun. Bags were packed, and we headed to the trucking company to get everything into my truck. The trailer was already loaded as another driver had brought it into the yard for final delivery to Bakersfield. We loaded all our stuff into the truck, hooked up to the trailer, got the delivery paperwork, and were ready to roll.

We were scheduled to unload the meat in Bakersfield on Christmas morning. I guess the people in Bakersfield don't mind working on Christmas. Maybe because they will need more stuff the day after Christmas?

When we left Albuquerque that evening, it was about five degrees and was getting colder. Before we left, I checked the refer (the trailer's refrigeration unit) and it would not start. No problem, I told the company because it would not be a problem until we got to the deserts of California. I told the dispatcher we would get the refer going before we got to the warmer climate in California. We drove to Flagstaff, Arizona, and stopped at a truck stop just west of town on Interstate 40. I filled the truck with diesel and tried to get the refer unit to start. No luck at all. I went to the shop behind the truck stop and talked with the mechanic about the refer not starting. He told me to bring the truck around to the shop, and they would see what they could do to get it running. After looking at the engine on the refer, he said I don't think it is getting any fuel. We checked the diesel tank under the trailer and found the fuel had jelled up from the cold. They brought out a torch and heated the tank for about thirty minutes. Then heated the fuel lines to the engine until the thing finally started.

We took off for a warmer country in California. We turned west on Highway 58 at Barstow, California, stopped at a roadside park across from Edwards Air Force Base, and went to sleep for about three hours. When we got to Tehachapi, California, the sun was coming up, and we headed for Bakersfield. When we got to the edge of the mountains, we stopped and took a picture of the valley going into Bakersfield. Clear up here, but down in the valley, it was foggy, and I mean not just a little fog, but the stuff you can't see twenty feet in.

Dropping down the mountains towards Bakersfield and on the outskirts of town, we were down to twenty miles per hour because of the fog. This was not going to be fun finding the place we were to unload the meat. From the directions we had, which included the address, we tried to find the place. But in the fog, we couldn't see the buildings next to the street, much less an address on the buildings. I pulled into a parking lot, and we got out of the truck and walked to where we could see some buildings. When we got within about thirty feet of the building, we could see the numbers on it.

This place was only a block from the appointed delivery location! How we got that close I still don't know. Lucky, I guess. Then we drove down the parking lot or rather inched on down, and there it was. The warehouse people asked me how I found them. Braille, I told them, and they started laughing. The fog started lifting a little, and we backed into the dock to unload. When we were unloaded, I called the dispatcher, and he told me to go to the TA Truck Stop in Ontario, California, and call him back. We headed for the TA, and about three hours later, we arrived. I selected a good parking spot close to the truck stop entrance. We went into the truck stop and I called in again.

The dispatcher told me because it was Christmas day no loads were going anywhere for a couple of days. This was what we wanted to hear. The weekend was here, as well as Christmas, and we were going to see some of Los Angeles before Diana had to fly back to Albuquerque.

We called a car rental company at the airport in Ontario, and they delivered a rental car to us. It was a Ford Probe, which was known as the Spanish Corvette. We drove to downtown Los Angeles and took in all the sights. Then on to Long Beach where we found the Queen Mary and took a tour of this big ship. We drove to Hollywood and looked around a little there. And got an eye full of Californians and their exotic cars as we drove down Rodeo Drive in Beverly Hills. The retail shops and restaurants added to our amazement of this area of the US of A. We did a lot of gawking and laughing at what we saw, which was very different from the sights in New Mexico or any other state we have lived in.

Then we went on to Universal Studios. We found a nice Mexican food place and had dinner. We then walked around Universal Studios for a couple of hours and then drove back to the TA in Ontario for the night. We got up the next morning, had breakfast in the café, and got ready for the day with showers and all that business. Diana had to get to the airport so she could catch her flight back to Albuquerque that day. She took the rental car back and flew back home that afternoon. So much for the Christmas vacation but we had fun and got to see some of Los Angeles. Most truck drivers don't do this sort of thing, but sometimes you must go for the gusto when you can. It was a good time, and I will miss having her in my truck sleeper at night.

I picked up a load of veggies just north of Los Angeles headed for Houston, Texas, after the little Christmas vacation with my wife, Diana. After unloading in Houston, I called in. The dispatcher told me they had a load of computers going to Washington, DC. Okay.

I asked where I would pick up the load and was told it was about fifty miles north of Houston at Compaq Computers. The dispatcher then tells me not many of their drivers would get this load.

He went on to say I got this load because I was a very careful driver.

I head out and get to the appointed pickup location. This area was very large and looked like something this cowboy had never seen before. There were about fifty buildings in this industrial complex. I have never seen anything so clean, ever. The lawns looked like they were mowed every day and the bushes were trimmed to perfection like they hired a barber to cut the shrubs. Wow, this is the cleanest place I have ever seen. That makes me think there must have been something left out in my upbringing. I think to myself that I must get out more

110

often. There is not even a cigarette butt anywhere to be found. I don't know how many people it takes to build these computers, but the janitorial staff must be in the hundreds.

I find the building marked "C" and go inside. This young lady at the reception desk looks at the load papers and directs me to a building marked "J," and sure enough, they have loading docks. I back into door number seven and ring the buzzer next to the door. The door opened, and I was once again amazed. It is the cleanest darn place I have ever seen. The people inside are all wearing white with little white caps and white shoes. I look at myself and wonder if they will let me in with jeans and cowboy boots on. They have thought of this and have a room for the slightly soiled truck drivers to stay while they load my trailer.

When I got the load instructions, I was told by the dispatcher to stop on the way to the computer company and have my truck washed.

The trailer also needed a thorough cleaning inside and out. I just hope to God there is not a stray carrot or leaf of lettuce in the trailer. I think these guys would have a fit. Sure enough, one of the workers walks into the trailer and has the look of someone trying to find veggie residue with a fine-tooth comb. He is wearing white gloves, of course, and comes out of the trailer holding a leaf of lettuce with his arm fully extended. I am now thinking I might be charged with veggie residue or something worse. He deposits the offending lettuce leaf into a small bin with a lid on it. Now I am really impressed. I think to myself, *"What if a driver came in with cow manure on his boots? Are these people going to faint or something worse?"*

I am finally loaded, and one of the warehouse fellows brings me the paperwork. He tells me the load I am carrying is worth about one and a half million dollars, so be careful. I tell the fellow I have not had a wreck in over a month, not to worry.

111

He gives me a stern look, and I just smile and make a hasty retreat. These computers are to unload in Washington, DC, on January 2nd.

I get to the appointed place to unload, and it is four-thirty in the afternoon of December 31st. This building has a sign in front which reads "U.S. Government." It is the size of a football field with a ten-foot fence and a guard gate in the driveway. The guard instructs me to unhook the trailer and come back on January 2nd at 9:00 a.m. He tells me about a small truck stop around the corner from there where I can park until I come back to put my trailer into the dock to unload.

I get to the truck, stop, and park. I find they have a nice café and showers. I look across the street and see a nightclub. I asked the girl behind the fuel counter about the place across the street. She tells me it is a nice club and might be a good place to go because they are having a New Year's Eve party, starting at nine. Great, I will get something to eat, take a shower, go to the place, and see what might be going on.

I go into the café, have a good fried chicken dinner, then take a shower, and put on the best jeans I have and a western shirt and cowboy boots. Most truck drivers don't have evening clothes suitable for Washington, DC, in their trucks. Well, I decided to go anyway. What the heck? I once was a sort of Bureaucrat four years earlier, in another life. I worked for a sub-agency of HUD in Durant, Oklahoma. I was head of the finance department, and in the fall of 1985, I was asked to go to Washington to write a speech for a Senator, which was to be given to a joint session of Congress.

My wife and I stayed at a hotel in Baltimore. There was to be a conference at the hotel, and the company wanted us to attend while we were there.

That evening, there was a party at the same hotel for some of the people from HUD, and we were invited to come.

Thinking this was going to be a fancy dinner and party, we dressed for the occasion. When we got to the dinner, the folks from HUD were the worst-dressed people I had ever seen. The girl sitting next to Diana was wearing jeans with half of the cheek of her butt showing through the hole in her jeans. Believe it or not, she was one of the best-dressed of the Washington crowd.

I walked across the street to the nightclub dressed in a western shirt, cowboy boots, and jeans. When I got inside, I felt like Jed Clampett at a Beverly Hills party. There were a couple of Senators, three or four congressmen, and many other bureaucrats in the place. There was even a fellow who I think was the ambassador to Mongolia. He was the coldest fellow I have ever tried to talk to. These folks must have been all Democrats, and since Bush was the president, they were not invited to the White House for the New Year's Eve party. These people were the most unfriendly folks I have ever been around. I had a drink at the bar, then went back to the truck stop to party with people that I could actually talk to.

The next day was January 1st, so I sat in the truck stop lounge, watched the football games, and visited with all the other truckers who were in the same state of waiting that I was in.

The next day, I got the computers unloaded and called the dispatcher to find out where I might be going from here. The dispatcher told me to go to Philadelphia to pick up a load of Chinese wedding baskets going to Denver, Colorado. The instructions as to how to get to the warehouse in Philadelphia took three pages of my notebook. I was told there were only certain streets I could take because the warehouse was in the old downtown area of Philadelphia. He told me most of the overpasses in the area are only about ten feet of clearance. The trailer was thirteen and a half feet tall.

He also said the streets in the area were built for horse-drawn carts. A big truck would have barely enough room to get down these streets, so don't make any mistakes. Not to worry, I told him. I am good at this and could drive anywhere. He just laughed at my remarks and said, "Be careful."

I drove to Philadelphia and found the warehouse with the wedding baskets. The street was as narrow as I was warned about, and no place to park something this big. The gate was closed at the warehouse and I would need to wait until the next morning at nine a.m. to load the baskets.

This was going to be a problem as there was no parking anywhere that I could see. I put my blinkers on, got out of the truck, and walked over to the warehouse to look at the place. This warehouse was old, and I mean really old. As I was headed back to the truck, along came a police car, and he stopped. The police officer asked me where I was to load, and I pointed at the warehouse across the street. He asked me when I would be loading. I told him it would be in the morning and that I was not sure where I could park for the night. The policeman then told me he would stop traffic so I could back up far enough to pull my truck onto the sidewalk next to that building there, he pointed. "Really?" I asked, "Parking on the sidewalk will not be a problem?" He told me that if I was gone by nine-thirty in the morning, it would be fine. This sort of thing goes on around here all the time because of the narrow streets and no parking close by.

The cop blocked the traffic, and I backed up and pulled the big Kenworth onto the sidewalk as close as I could next to the building. By then, it was about six-thirty in the evening. I got out of the truck and walked to the end of the block. There was a little store there, sort of like a 7-11 store. I went inside and found they had deli sandwiches. When I went to pay for the food, the fellow behind the counter asked me where I was from. "Albuquerque, New Mexico," I answered. He then asked me if

I had to have a green card to get into the United States. "Well, no sir," I said. I explained that New Mexico was the state next to Texas and Arizona. He still looked like he wasn't sure about that and was staring at me really hard as I went out the door. Geography must not have been one of his better subjects when he was in school. I would guess this fellow to be about seventy years old and I doubt he has ever been out of the city.

The next morning, with no coffee, I walk around for about an hour until I see the gate opening across the street at the warehouse. I walk over and find there is an office building in the corner of the place. I went inside. This was about eight-thirty and only two people were there as yet. I tell them that I am to pick up a load of wedding baskets at 9:00 a.m. The fellow asked me where my truck was. I told him I was parked across the street, next to an office building. We go outside and look at my truck. "Wow," the fellow says to me, "We have a new girl in the office and she didn't know we usually send our big loads to a distribution house which is about eight miles north of here. She didn't know that and arranged for your company to send a truck here." He just shook his head in amazement.

This warehouse was built in 1861, and I think they didn't have trucks that big back then. I agreed with him and asked what shall we do now that I'm here? By this time there were four other cars parked in front of the office. I tell the guy, "Let's go look at the size of the place."

We go back outside and start looking. At the street, there is a brick fence about eight feet tall, and we walk over to the gate. I tell him I will walk off the lot, and I think I will be able to tell whether I can get in here or not. We start walking around the lot, and I tell the guy if you can move all the cars parked in front of the office and block the streets for about five minutes, I think I can back into the place and get the trailer into one of the docks.

115

Now, there were about eight people in the office, and they were all looking at my truck across the street. They are all shaking their heads and all talking at once. I tell them, "We won't know if it can be done unless I give it a try." Now, they are all talking at the same time, and we decide to give it a try.

The head chief of the place calls the police and asks if they could send a couple of squad cars and block off the street. The two police cars arrive, and I show them where we need the streets blocked. One of the officers was a sergeant, and he tells the other one to get behind the truck and block that street. He told me he would go around the corner and block that street. He told two of the fellows in the office to go just beyond the gate and stop all the cars coming from that direction.

We all get to our places, and I get into the truck and pull back into the street. I get to the corner where the little store is, turn to the right, and then stop with the back of the trailer straight across the street from the warehouse gate. I start backing up and get the trailer through the gate at a slight angle to the left. Just as the truck cleared the gate, I turned and jackknifed the trailer to the left, then back to the right. How I got the trailer to the dock is a wonder to this day. We opened the trailer doors, and I backed up six more feet and hit the dock square. All eight of the warehouse folks were standing at the front of the office, applauding when I got out of the cab. Seven of the warehouse workers were giving one of the gals five bucks each. I walked over, and they were all shaking their heads and saying that was the best driving they had ever seen. I asked, "Why were all you guys giving this girl money?" She was the only one of the eight that had bet on me. The rest of the warehouse folks didn't think I could get the truck into the dock. "Well," I said, "I was not sure it could be done either, but if I didn't try, we would never know."

Two of the guys tell me to come with them, and they will show me the warehouse part of the building. I follow them to the stairs leading to the dock, and then we go inside. *Wow, this place is old,* I think to myself, and then they take me to the elevator to the second floor. I tell the fellows I didn't know they had elevators in 1861. Well, the building had an elevator, all right, and when the guys closed the door and started pulling on a big rope, I was amazed. The darn thing went to the second floor, and when they opened the door, there must have been fifty thousand wedding baskets in the place.

They got the trailer loaded, and I had to wait for a UPS truck to get out of the lot before I tried to move the big Kenworth. I turned right some more, closed the doors on the trailer, and pulled up to where the front bumper of the Kenworth was about a foot from the office door. I had to back up and turn three or four times to get straight enough to get the thing out of their gate.

I finally get the truck out of town and head for Denver, Colorado. Two days later, I arrived at the appointed place to deliver the wedding baskets, and it started snowing. It was about nine in the evening when I got to Denver, so when I arrived at the warehouse to unload, it was ten-thirty, and now it was really snowing. I see the warehouse has a security guard; I go inside and tell him that I have a load of wedding baskets. He looks at his paperwork and says that I am at the right place and I am scheduled to unload at eight in the morning. "Great," I tell him. I told him I had stopped at a place and got some sandwiches, so I would go eat them and go to bed.

I walk back to the truck, get in, and start to have the tasty repast when I see in the mirror a fellow walking beside my trailer towards the cab. The guy gets to the cab of the truck and motions me to roll my window down. I asked him what he wanted, and he said: "Are you here to unload?" "Yes," I told him. I thought he was with the warehouse. He then started telling me his car had broken down and asked if I could help him out a little. It was still snowing, and I wasn't going to get out in the snow to see what might be wrong with his car. I felt like I was getting a cold or flu, so I didn't want to go out in the snow and cold. I told the guy this, and he seemed to get angry. Then he said, "Why don't you give me all your money?" and pulled a large knife from his jacket. In my briefcase, I had my Smith and Wesson .357 magnum pistol. The briefcase was in the passenger seat, and I pulled the gun out while pulling the hammer back. I pointed it at the guy and said, "I don't think so." He started running toward the street, and in a couple of seconds, he was out of sight with the snow coming down now very hard.

I just sat there and waited for a while and was looking around but didn't see the fellow again. I put my coat back on and the pistol in my belt and climbed down from the cab of my truck. Looking all around very carefully, I headed for the security guard's office in the warehouse. I told the guard about what had just happened, and he called the police. In a few minutes, a squad car pulled up, and two officers came into the guard's office. I told them about what had happened, and they told me that two guys had been robbed in this area just yesterday. They told me to lock my doors, and they would drive around and look for this guy. I didn't hear from them again that night. I had gone back to the truck and went to bed. When I got up in the morning, the snow had stopped, and the sun was shining. I got unloaded and called the dispatcher. He told me that I was to pick up a load of cheese there in Denver that would unload in Albuquerque.

I got the cheese and headed south on Interstate 25. Once the cheese was unloaded, I called and told the dispatcher that I was getting sick and wanted a few days off to heal up.

That winter I drove over most of the mountain passes that are on interstate highways in the country. Many of them had snow or ice and fog on them. One night, after loading a full trailer of chocolate rabbits in St Albans, Vermont, bound for

Walmart in Plainview, Texas, I got in one heck of a snowstorm in upstate New York.

I left St Albans at about four in the evening and had to go north to where I could cross Lake Champlain into New York State. The highway is two-lane, and it goes from island to island to get across the lake. I figured I was nearly across the lake when, on one of the islands, there was an underpass with a sign on the top that said "Clearance 12'4."

I hit the brakes, stopped, and got out my map to see if there was another road. There wasn't another road or even a cow trail. I backed up along the side of the road for about a quarter of a mile until I could see a place big enough for me to turn around. There was a convenience store a little further back on the road, and I headed to it. I got out of the truck and walked to the store.

When I walked in, the girl behind the counter didn't even wait for me to say a word. She told me that I would be clear and I should go on. I told her my trailer was 13'6" and the sign read 12'4." She said the sign is for the ice that will form under the bridge. Now, without the ice, my trailer will clear it. She explained, "A thousand trucks have stopped here and we tell them all the same thing, and they all make it to the other side without ripping off the top foot of their trailers."

About that time, another truck came along and didn't even slow down. I know that one was as tall as my trailer, so I figured I might as well take a chance. Sure enough, I made it just fine and went on into the State of New York.

I turn south on Interstate 87 and think I will cover a pretty good distance before I get some sleep. I didn't go fifty miles until it started to snow, and I was heading into the mountains. By the time I was in the highest part of these hills, called the Adirondacks, the snow was eight inches deep, and not a snowplow in sight. The chocolate rabbits only weighed

119

about sixteen thousand pounds, and that gave me very good traction without being overly heavy. I buzzed right along at about fifty miles per hour all the way across these hills. It was about midnight, and there was no traffic at all. Seems like most people had the good sense not to be out here on a night like this.

I go to about eighty or ninety miles from Albany when this screwball in a Jeep CJ comes out to play. I guess he figured with no one out here he could play in the snow on the interstate highway. Well, he finally looked in his mirror and saw me coming up to him. He about had an accident, and I don't mean with the Jeep; I mean in the Jeep. He couldn't get out of the way fast enough to suit him and he started sliding from side to side. I had already figured out he wasn't looking for me, and I thought I had better look out for him. I slowed to about fifteen miles an hour, and he saw I wasn't going to run him over. He tried to lead foot it out of there, and he did—for a little way, anyhow. He got about half a mile ahead of me and started to play again, and this time, he did it. Slid right off into the ditch on the right and it was a deep one. I slowed up again, and as I went by, he was spinning all four tires, trying to get the Jeep to move. I do hope he made it out before the spring thaw.

φ

I look out the window of the airplane and we are coming in over the Manzano Mountains just east of Albuquerque, America. Oh, Honey! I'm almost home, and I sure hope my wife is at the airport to pick me up. What a trip this has been, one I shall never forget.

My wife is there to get me, and I sure am glad to be home, even if it is in Albuquerque.

Chapter Thirteen

After a few days at home and after talking it over with my wife, I decided to drive to Las Vegas, Nevada, and look around for a few days. I stopped on Fremont Street in Vegas and saw a sign on a building that said International Dealers School. I went in and talked to the head of the school and found out that if I was currently unemployed, I could get a grant to pay for this course. When I got back to Albuquerque, Diana and I talked about moving to Las Vegas. I was done driving the big rigs for a while, and maybe being a dealer in Vegas was the right thing to do.

I went back to Vegas the day after Labor Day and started the dealer's school the following Monday. I rented an apartment that was very reasonable in price, and it was behind Sam's Town. I had figured out I could live in Vegas very inexpensively if I was careful. In 1992, this apartment was less than $500 per month, and I could eat for about five dollars a day. I could and did make over twenty-five dollars per day playing blackjack. I knew and have found quickly that very few people could do this every day. I did this every day for over a month. This made me over $750 the first month I lived in Las Vegas.

I had started the dealers' school, which was only five days per week, Monday through Friday. I was looking for something else to do in addition to attending the sixteen-week school. Diana was still in Albuquerque and getting ready to move at the end of the year. So, I had time on my hands but didn't want to be foolish enough to believe I could be a professional gambler and consistently make money every day. I needed a job of some sort.

One day, I was looking in the local newspaper and saw an ad for an instructor for a truck driving school. With an address in hand, I decided to go check this out and found the location of the school. I talked to the head of the school and got hired as an instructor for the evening class. The dealers' school ended at four in the afternoon, and the truck driving evening class started at five. Instructing future truck drivers in this class ended at one in the morning. This gave me plenty of time to get some sleep before going to the dealers' school. Well, this would work out just fine. I would make enough to pay my rent, food, and all other expenses.

The truck driving class was a six-week course.

In the end, the new truck driver would be certified and get a CDL license. The classroom portion of the school was just south of downtown Las Vegas. The driving portion was at a location just off Interstate 25 on the northeast side of Vegas.

The driving school had a manager and three instructors. The number of students we had in the hands-on driving part of the class was large enough for each instructor to have three students for half of the time. Then, for the other half of their time in the hands-on class, these students were taught how to maintain the trucks. So, each night I had a total of six students who I taught, five days each week.

The manager of this school had over twenty-five years driving an over-the-road truck. The other two instructors also had many years of driving. I had lots of years of experience driving just about every kind of truck out there. If it had wheels and a steering wheel, I could drive it, and I started when I was around fourteen years old. Unlike the manager, my experience wasn't consistent over many years, but I was good at it and knew I could teach others to be successful professional truck drivers.

The trucks we used in the hands-on driving part of the school were International Cabovers. Most of the over-the-road trucks of today are the long-nose type seen every day going down the road. The flat nose trucks are still used in Europe and Asia but not so much here in this country. We have bigger highways than in Europe and Asia, and the long-nose trucks ride better. I guess that is why most of the American trucking companies have gone to this type of rig.

In the first class of students I taught at the drivers' school, there was a fellow who was six foot ten inches tall. He was an All-American basketball player in college. He was drafted by the Phoenix Suns but didn't make the cut. He played in Italy for three years before an injury ended his career in basketball.

One of the students was just twenty-one and thought he was going to be the best driver in the world. This kid had an attitude. He thought he knew everything there was to know about driving a big truck. The first week he was in the class, I told him to show me just how well he could drive. Talk is one thing, and driving a big truck is another. He could not shift the gears without grinding every one of them. I tried talking to him and showing him how the gears shifted with a ten-speed road ranger. It takes practice, I would tell all of them. Then, I would get behind the wheel and shift every gear without using the clutch. If it is done right, you don't need the clutch except to start and stop. This kid could not get the concept of how to do the shifting in this manner.

Finally, on the fourth night of school, it was his turn to be the next driver. He got behind the wheel at the schoolyard. I told the students we would be going north on Interstate 25 and then turn north on the road to Alamo, Nevada. We got to the intersection that was next to the interstate and stopped at the red light. I was telling the students about how you needed to get the RPM at the shift point then as the RPM dropped, the shifter would go into the next gear without the clutch. This was a concept which only a few could get into their heads. I told them this takes practice to master, and we are going to practice until it comes naturally to you.

Jimmy could not get the ten-speed road ranger into gear. He got very mad and was cussing and yelling about the truck. I explained to him it was not the truck's fault; it was your fault for thinking you knew how it was done with no experience. Well, he got even madder when I said that to him. I told Jimmy to get out, and I put another driver in behind the wheel. I told Jimmy to get into the sleeper or walk the mile back to the truck yard. We were sitting in the middle of the intersection when all this happened. Jimmy finally got into the cab, and we started off again.

The guy who I put into the driver's seat to take over the driving had a little bit of experience but had not gotten a CDL license—Commercial Drivers' License. The only companies that would hire someone without a CDL that I knew of were in other states. The nearest one was in Salt Lake City, Utah. His only option was to go to a driving school where he could get his CDL.

I told them we would go to Apex and turn north on the highway to Alamo. During the daytime, there is only about one car every ten minutes on this highway, and this was about nine in the evening. At this hour, we would probably see about one car every twenty minutes, so we could do about anything we wanted on this road. I told the guy driving to go through all the gears, then downshift to a stop, and then start over. He did this about two times, and I told the third guy it was his turn to do the same thing. When we traded drivers, I got into the sleeper with Jimmy.

I asked Jimmy what he wanted to do and if he had thought during the last thirty minutes about the problem he had and the scene he had created. He had calmed down by then and told me he was sorry about all that had happened. He told me he would listen to me and my instructions.

He added that he really wanted to learn to drive the big trucks.

I then told the three students the story about when I was in high school, and my dad bought the first big cattle trailer. I told them about my trying to back the thing into a cattle shoot without much luck and the cowboys laughing at me for my inexperience. When we got back home, I told my mother that would be the last time someone would laugh at me for the way I drove a big truck. This story made them all laugh. Then I told them that by the time you three guys graduate, no one will laugh at you either. When you get your CDL, you will be able to not only drive one of these things, you will be able to get back into any dock in the country. I then looked at Jimmy and said, "Son, I have nothing against you at all, and I want you to be the best you can be, not only in driving but in everything you do. It starts with the attitude that you believe you are going to be the best you can be at anything you try. To be a good truck driver, you must be good at many other things, too. I will be talking about these other things in the next six weeks so much you will be glad to be rid of me when you graduate."

I then said, "For the next thirty minutes, Jimmy, I don't want you to look at anything but the driver's feet on the clutch and gas pedal. Then you are going to drive us back to Las Vegas and you are going to do it very well if you will just listen to me." Jimmy said he was sorry and that he wanted very much to be a good driver.

Well, to make a long story short, not only did he learn, but when he graduated, he was hired by the Jack B. Kelly Company in Amarillo, Texas. This company I knew quite a bit about and they did not hire drivers that were rookies, so to speak. Jimmy became that good and we had a good time the next five weeks. We would go to a new commercial building with loading docks in the back which had not been moved into yet. It had a big parking lot in the back with two loading docks. This was perfect to practice backing the big trucks with a fifty-three-foot trailer. Jimmy became a model student and learned all that I could teach him. I hope he is still out there on the road, making a good living and having fun doing it.

Each week, some students would graduate, and each Monday, we would get some new ones. We had five tractors and five trailers that were fifty-three feet long. We also had a set of doubles that we would take out one evening each week. I took my students to places that most of the other instructors would not.

We went to the Hoover Dam. The road from Vegas to the dam was not the best in the country. It was steep and windy and had only two lanes at the time. Today, there is a four-lane and a new bridge that goes across the Black Canyon just about a mile from the Hoover Dam. But this was in 1992, and it was not the easiest drive, but it would teach the students about the roads they would encounter out there on the highways and byways in the United States. There are hills in California as well as in other states like Colorado. You better know how to drive if you want to get old enough to retire someday. My dad would say you can go down a hill a thousand times too slow but only one too fast.

We got a new student one Monday who was a twenty-eight-year-old lady who never had a driver's license of any kind. She had just married a truck driver, and they were going to drive as a team for a company out of Springfield, MO. She needed to have a CDL to do this.

The Monday she started at the school, the manager asked who wanted this lady. The other two instructors said,

"Not me." I spoke up and said, "I will take her because she has no bad habits to break to become a truck driver." The other two instructors, when they thought about what I said, told the manager they would take her. The manager said to them, "You had your chance and missed it."

Well, I was right, and in two weeks, she drove a set of doubles over Hoover Dam. She was the easiest student I had while I worked there. She had no bad habits to break; she wanted to learn, and she did just that. I gave all the students the same speech I gave to Jimmy about being the best you can be at anything you try to do. Well, this worked like a charm with her, as well as most of the students I had there.

I did have one guy who flunked because he did not listen to anyone at the school. After three weeks, he still could not even get one of the big trucks out of the parking lot. We instructors did everything we could to teach him. At the end of three weeks of his schooling, we voted to kick him out and told the school to give him his money back, which they did.

Chapter Fourteen

Before going to Las Vegas, I started writing down the events I had written in my diary and filled in with other remembrances of my truck driving career.

And ol' Le Roy retired to sitting on top of my file cabinet in my office while I composed my story. He is content to just sit there in silence and observe all that goes on around him. Besides, he is convalescing from an elongated head from being hung from the roof of the truck by a bungee cord for fifty thousand miles.

Le Roy is from California, and as you might have guessed by now, the reason for the purple color is that he is a raisin. I won Le Roy at the state fair in 1988. He is a little larger than a grapefruit and a little smaller than a soccer ball. He has short little legs with red tennis shoes. His arms look just like his legs except for the red Reeboks. His arms have little hands at the ends.

Yea, little Le ROY, excuse me, the Reverend Le Roy Ras'on, as he has been dubbed, has traveled a lot of miles and seen a lot of strange sights in the last two years.

Le Roy has confided in me some things about the trucking industry that he thinks you should know.

Once upon a time, the way the heck back there, there were truckers. Thousands of years ago, they were the camel jockeys in the caravans who transported goods from the east to what was considered the civilized part of the world.

Then there were the men who walked along with the ox carts with solid wooden wheels that moved civilization to Europe and then to America.

They were the teamsters that, in our early times, moved the freight to make America grow and prosper. These brave and solitary men endured many hardships to deliver their loads to an untamed land. I believe they are the essence of the modern-day road cowboy. These were men who were independent, lonely, strong and, in many instances, willing to go against what common sense teaches is safe. They had a desire to succeed even at the risk of losing their lives. I don't believe history has given them their just due.

Yes, everything we have, our food, our clothing and almost everything else, has been delivered to us by trucks. In these times of fast cars, faster living, and even faster news coverage, I think we forget how we get what we have.

I remember a story I heard a few years ago which goes like this. A person in New York was asked what she thought about the plight of the dairy farmer. Her reply was, "What do I care about the dairy farmer? I get my milk at the supermarket." I hope we are not all of this mind. We would be in real trouble if this were the case. But do we really think about how all of our stuff gets to us?

This country went from the teamster to the train in the mid to late nineteenth century. We grew and prospered as a nation, and the teamster was reduced to doing a delivery job. The products of the Industrial Revolution were moved by train and then delivered to their final destination by wagon. The teamster became a short-haul trucker.

As the years went by, many changes also befell the train. The country went through a depression, and many a train and their tracks also became depressed. How many old and nonrepairable tracks have been turned into private land and have been made into landscaping ornaments in the last fifty years?

As a child in Fredrick, Oklahoma, I remember a train that went by the name of the FBS&T— "try weekly." That stood for the Fredrick, Burt Spur, and Tipton Rail Road. "Try weekly" meant that it tried to get to Tipton one week and then tried to get back to Fredrick the next week. Not bad, for it is only fifteen to eighteen miles one way. In bursts of speed, it could hit two or three miles an hour. This is with only one stop in the middle, Burt Spur.

Well, one day, it just quit trying, and now there is just a slight rise in the old dirt road that is a quarter of a mile south of our old home place, where the FBS&T once carried its freight in all its glory. It may surprise you to know there are still people living in those little places today. The railroad is gone, along with many others, just like it is in thousands of places all over the country.

These people still eat and have almost the same things they have always had. They just get their goods by truck now. I will also bet they have fewer gardens now than thirty years ago, and most don't have a chicken, a hog or a bovine critter in the place.

I have a friend who lives in Chicago who is my age. He told me he has never raised a garden, punched a cow, or hog, and he said he has never missed a meal yet. I will bet that most of his stuff came by truck also.

The point I am trying to make is this. If the railroads have faded in prominence in the movement of what we use every day of our lives, then how do we get all we have? By truck, that's how. They are on every highway and byway in the nation. Every type of truck, from big rigs to large cars and delivery vans, has increased in numbers over the past forty years. They have evolved over the years in the same manner the automobile has.

The driver is in a better-riding, more comfortable truck with hundreds of amenities. The teamster of old would never have dreamed of such comfort.

The big rigs in the old days were the twenty-mule teams. This was a twenty-horsepower vehicle with an attitude problem. Some of the modern trucks have up to six hundred horsepower, and most of the time the only attitude problem lies with the driver.

Now, let's talk a little about the types and kinds of big rigs you might see out there on the highway. There are a lot of smaller trucks running around, but I will not go into them much except to say there are a lot of smaller trucks running around on the roads.

The big rig comes in basic flavors: the cab over and the conventional. The cabover is the flat-nosed truck, which derives its name from the fact the cab is on top of the engine. The conventional is the truck with the long hood. Now, the latest of the conventional ones have a slanted hood. With the ever-increasing cost of fuel, the truck manufacturers decided a more aerodynamic design was needed to increase fuel efficiency. The T600 Kenworth was the first of this new breed of truck. Now, almost all of the big truck makers have their version of the "anteater" style of hood. To be very honest, it is the newer and better engines that have contributed to fuel efficiency far more than the sloped nose. Air shields on the top of the cabs have also done a lot for better fuel mileage.

The prominent brands of big trucks are the Kenworth and Peterbilt, built by PACCAR; the Freightliner, owned by Daimler Benz; the International, built by Navistar; the Western Star, Marmon; the Ford-built by Henry and Co.; the White

Volvo GMC and the Mack. The new ones will range in cost from fifty to one hundred thousand dollars each.

You can get engines built by Cummins, Caterpillar, Detroit Diesel Corporation and Mack, ranging in horsepower from two hundred seventy to four hundred sixty. Transmissions come from Eaton, Rockwell and Spicer, with the number of forward gears from five to twenty-four. The more popular ones now are the nine-speed, thirteen-speed and fifteen-speed from Eaton. These transmissions are referred to as the Fuller Road Rangers.

You can get springs under your buns all the way to an eight-bag air ride. The cabs also may be air ride. The sleepers can range from a thirty-six-inch box all the way to the Aerodyne type with sixty inches or more of pure luxury. Some come with double bunks, their own heat and air and space for everything from a lazy boy recliner to a TV with a VCR. The home away from home.

My dad drove a truck in the 1930s that had no sleeper, sixty-five horsepower, and the ride - well, he said the truck was christened by Teddy Roosevelt for it was a rough-riding son of a gun. He hauled cotton bales from Oklahoma to Houston, Texas. Sometimes not getting any sleep for three days. I, to be honest, don't know how he did it and has lived to be seventy-nine, so far.

The "large car" or "big truck," as they are known, usually are the owner-operators. These are the ones with the big horsepower, the shiny wings on the tops of the cabs, and some claims are the triple-digit trucks. That means they will go over a hundred miles an hour in the big hole—top gear. I have heard all my life about these fast trucks but have seen only a very few that would really do the 115 or 125 mph claimed by some. Some readers of this will probably say, why that fool writer should see my truck! It will do 130 mph uphill with a load, in the rain, with two gears left and so on.

With all these improvements in the equipment over the years, the life of the truck driver should have improved as well. It has to the extent that the truck itself is a better piece of machinery. The driver still has many of the same problems they have had since the first camel caravans crossed the deserts of the Middle East.

The modern-day truck driver, like his counterpart of old, is still independent and has a desire to do things for himself. He is still leading a lonely existence, one that changes constantly with every mile he drives. One day, he can be in a warm, humid climate on a highway surrounded by forested hills, and the next day be crossing the arid deserts of the Southwest.

The long-haul driver calls his family to let them know where he is today. He tells them he is still doing okay and that he is well. His voice usually will not project the loneliness he feels, knowing he has to hang up the phone in a few minutes and be on his way. He will hear the problems of home but can only be able to make recommendations for their cure. He is on his way to California or Florida and has problems of his own to worry about. He will be understanding and know in his mind he is not there to see all that is going on. But he is a trucker, and he must deliver the load, then go where his company dispatches him. If he is lucky, he can run by the house on his next load unless he has trouble somewhere and doesn't have the time. Most long-haul drivers are barely able to get to the house once a month, then only for a day or two.

With the increase in the number of trucks on the road over the past thirty or forty years, many a problem has befallen the trucking industry. Finding quality drivers is an ever-increasing problem. It takes a special sort of person. Nowadays, a lot of women are becoming drivers.

Being a truck driver means leaving the security of home and roaming the highways of America. Being gone from home is just one of the ills that must be overcome.

The modern-day long-haul driver has to abide by all sorts of rules and regulations enforced by a variety of agencies. He must abide by state, federal, and local laws, and the infamous DOT. These are the guys truck drivers dislike about as bad as the highway patrol.

In some states, they are even worse than the state cops. The DOT has a rulebook that is written in pure "lawyer." The rules concerning the driver's logbook are long and complicated, and in most of the drivers' minds, the logbook is the worst offender in the world. A driver can't drive but ten hours per every twenty-four. I have often wondered how many people who are in business for themselves would go broke if they only worked ten hours per day.

I believe I could write the entire rules concerning the driver's logbook in one sentence. It would be as follows: "No Driver shall be on duty or drive more than fourteen hours per twenty-four hours." You would not need to say any more about the logbook than that. I believe most people could not go at it for more than the fourteen-hour limit, day after day. This would make it necessary for the government to eliminate a great many rules and the people to enforce them. But they wouldn't do that now, would they?

I drove from Nogales, Arizona, to Boston in three days. The trip is about twenty-five hundred miles, and with the limit of ten hours or about six hundred miles per day, the trip should have taken two or three days longer. Drivers can't make any money if they play by the rules all the time. Does this make them bad guys or outlaws? I think not. I believe they are, for the most part, just trying to feed their families and maybe get ahead in the game so that when they get caught by the DOT, they will have enough money to pay their fine.

Maybe all truck drivers could confess and become wards of the government. Another five or six million mouths to feed could help the farmers out because the government gets most of the stuff anyway. But that is another problem, and I am only interested in solving one major problem at a time.

Heck, all the drivers could become Democrats and run for Congress just before we all starve to death. This could also ruin the manufacturing of Harley-Davidson Tee Shirts.

I once picked up a load of paper in Warwick, New York, that was to be delivered to El Paso, Texas. Upon arrival at the appointed destination, I ran out of hours in my logbook. One cannot drive but seventy hours in an eight-day period. After leaving El Paso for Carlsbad, New Mexico, I knew I would need to be careful not to be stopped because of the logbook problem.

I went through the New Mexico port of entry and weigh station without being checked. I got to just the other side of town when a DOT roadblock stopped me. The DOT officer asked me for my load papers and the truck registration. I smiled and gave him the truck papers and told him I was empty. He then asked me for my logbook. I gave this to him also and told him it was up to date and in good shape. He looked the logbook over very carefully and said, "It is in good shape except for one thing. You ran out of hours about thirty minutes ago."

I then said, "I realize that, but this is a minor indiscretion that I feel you should overlook because I am just going to the salt mine, which is about three miles further down the road."

He said, "It is not three miles; it is thirteen miles." I then told him I would hurry. I am not sure what he was thinking, but he just looked up at me, gave me back my book and truck papers, and told me to get out of there.

I promptly complied and drove to the salt mine, got a load of salt in about an hour and a half and drove to Tucumcari, New Mexico. I unloaded the salt then drove to Friona, Texas, got a load of boxed meat, and did not stop until I got home in Albuquerque, New Mexico. When I got home, I had to take two days off so my logbook could catch up with me.

If I had been caught somewhere around Santa Rosa, New Mexico, that night, I think I would have had to plead insanity to the charges and fall upon the mercy of the court to be able to write this book without being in jail.

Even though I was rather tired, I had been gone from home for a couple of weeks. I didn't want to stay within shouting distance from home and wait another two days to get there.

I often wonder where the trucking industry is going to get enough drivers to fill the empty spots created by the new Commercial Driver's License. It will, in my opinion, cause about twenty to twenty-five percent of all truck drivers to try something else to make a living. Some of them might even become car salesmen or worse. This new license was designed to find drivers with more than one state driver's license and find out how much each and every driver knows about his brakes. I feel this is important to know because if the driver doesn't know enough about the brakes on his truck, he might not be able to find the right pedal to apply this safety device, and we would have too many tomatoes in Hawaii. This would cause the price of coconuts to drop, and the domino effect of that could be devastating to the world economy. Not to mention, all the parking spaces would be taken, and the tourists would have no place to park their rental cars.

If all the drivers of trucks in the country followed the DOT rules to the letter, most of them would be homeless. Then look what that would do to the budget the current congress has worked so hard on to get under control—NOT. This is a joke. The truck stops would be full of trucks, with their drivers watching their clocks so they could go another ten hours.

I, along with most every other person of sound mind, need some rules to live by. I am not sure the drug pushers could make a decent living without them. I also believe all of the bureaucratic bull crap associated with the trucking industry does not always serve the best interest of the country. But there are a lot of wrongs in other industries as well. I think these will need to wait for the next book to be addressed properly.

I made a speech once while in the banking industry to a group of business leaders and public officials in Eastern Oklahoma. The speech was on economic development and my comments on what the state could do to realize a better future. After I finished talking, a group of these wise and noble leaders asked if I would be interested in running for Governor of the State. I thanked them for their offer and laughed to myself until leaving the place where the seminar was held and discussed this statement with my wife. I became very disheartened by the fact they would ask someone like me to run for Governor just for telling the truth without fear of offending any one person or group. Well, I want you to know I did the right thing; I quit making that kind of speech. I figured a person could get into all kinds of poo-poo by running for public office.

I was going to run for mayor of Gruver, Texas, once until I saw how many people voted in the last election. I thought if the current mayor only had twenty-four friends, he had to have over one thousand enemies. I wasn't ready for the abuse. Besides, the job only paid one hundred dollars a month and the mayor would need to be a better financial wizard than I to make a living on that amount of money. Another reason I didn't run was my age. I was only twenty-two years old and wanted to see my son grow up without being made fun of.

φ

I believe the driver problem will get worse before it gets better. Current unemployment and what is being called a recession could help driver recruiting. People are more willing to go on the road and to make a change when they are faced with poverty where they are.

Chapter Fifteen

Speaking of poverty, I should tell you about the money I have made, along with some of the real money that can be made in the trucking business.

I, like most drivers, have driven for either a company or an individual. Most drivers get paid by the mile. Some are paid a percentage of the load. I have been paid both ways.

The mileage pay generally ranges from seventeen cents per mile to around twenty-six cents. Some union companies will pay more. The percentages are usually twenty to twenty-five percent of the gross haul. Some companies will pay the drivers by the loaded mile. Some pay for all miles driven, and some for all miles driven according to the mover's guide.

The mover's guide is the shortest route between two points. Some of their roads are not fit for the big heavy haul trucks. I will not spend any time on owner-operators because their rate of pay, if I tried to list it all, would take up an entire book.

I know an owner-operator who, twenty years ago, bought his first truck and promptly got it repossessed. Somehow, he managed to hang on to his trailer and leased it to another owner-operator. Within a few years, this guy had over one hundred trailers and started to buy trucks again. A few years after that, he was worth millions and built a very fine trucking company in Milwaukee. Success can be obtained in the trucking business; just look at J.B. Hunt.

In 1970, I hauled cattle from the stockyards in Amarillo, Texas, to Colorado. Mostly just north of Denver to a town called Longmont. If you are a beer drinker, you should know the name Coors. A great many of the loads of heifers, young female bovines, I hauled went to Coors. Before you ask if cows are used in the making of beer, the answer is no. Coors is, or was, at that time, involved in the cattle business. At least, I don't think cow critters are used in the process of making beer. I lived in Milwaukee for a time and I never saw any cows hanging around the Miller Brewery. I think they may be used to stomp grapes from the taste of some wines I have tried, but not beer, to my knowledge, anyway.

As I said, I hauled these loads of cattle for a percentage of the revenue. I made about one hundred five dollars per load, which was twenty-five percent of the haul. I could make four to five loads per week. I think I was averaging five hundred per week in income. I would venture to say the average driver in 1991 made just about the same as I did in 1970.

One week in June of 1970 I made six trips to Colorado and made about eight hundred dollars. Most truck drivers can't make that in a week now. In 1970, eight hundred a week was a lot of money. I might also add to this story that after I made six, eight hundred-and-fifty-mile trips in one week, I slept for three days straight. I think I was totally unconscious for the first two of those days. Each trip took about twenty-one hours. I would only have time to go by the house in Amarillo to take a shower, change clothes, pat the wife on the rear, and kiss the kids.

The first week I did this kind of thing was in April of 1970. I left Amarillo on a Monday evening after the livestock auction closed and drove to Colorado with a load of steers. I got back to Amarillo about four the following afternoon and loaded another bunch of steers that evening around six-thirty. By the time I got to Lamar, Colorado I was so sleepy I was having a hard time staying on the road. There were seven trucks in our little convoy. All of us were headed for Coors, north of Denver. We stopped for coffee in Lamar, but that didn't help. Twenty miles north of town, I was having one hell of a time trying to stay awake. That's when I became acquainted with Uncle "Benny." The truck in front of me stopped and asked why I was weaving all over the road, and I told him this was the second trip without any sleep. He said I should try one of his little black pills. "What is it?" I asked. "Black Magic, Uncle Benny," was the reply. He told me one of these little varmints would take you to Denver and back two times.

Well, I took the thing, put a cigar in my mouth, and started driving. The next afternoon, about six, when I pulled into Amarillo again, I felt great. Hell, I didn't even stop to spit, and I still had the cigar in my mouth. I didn't remember a whole lot about the drive, but I must have had more fun than a barrel of monkeys. With another one of these little pills, I was ready to go again without any sleep whatsoever. I was going to make more money than I had ever done in my life. Yep, me and ol' Ben were going to do some serious trucking. Let's get them damn bovines on the truck and put aviator caps on them because we are going to fly. And fly we did until about midnight. I was slowing down for the little town of Wild Horse, Colorado, when I felt something shift in the back of the trailer. I pulled over and stopped to see what the trouble was. When I got to the back of the trailer, I could see one of the heifers had fallen from the jail to the bottom deck. The jail is the little compartment in the rear of the trailer on the upper right-hand side. I found an empty trailer in a parking lot and unloaded the cows from the rear of my truck. Then, I reloaded them the way they were before the high-jumping heifer made the swan dive to the bottom deck. When I unloaded the young ladies at the Coors feedlot, I was just hoping the acrobatic cow would be able to walk out on her own. She did.

I took another little pill and headed for Amarillo. I got home at about seven-thirty in the evening. I told my wife I was going to take a bath before I ate anything. I drank a tall glass of milk, not knowing it would kill the effect of the little pill, and climbed into the tub for a soak. Two hours later, my wife finally got me to wake up, and I got out of the water, all shriveled up like a prune. I was beginning to see there were some things about taking these pills that were not normal.

The next morning, I loaded another bunch of heifers for the journey to Colorado. I then made another trip, taking my brother-in-law with me. My brother-in-law was to be married in June of that year, so on the way back from Denver, we turned on Interstate 25 South. That highway took us to Colorado Springs, where the Broadmoor Hotel and Resort is located. We left the cattle trailer at a truck stop and drove to the Broadmoor to check it out. Bob wanted to go there on his honeymoon, and he had never been there before.

From the Broadmoor, we drove the tractor to Cheyenne Mountain to the entrance of the Will Rogers Memorial. There is a toll booth there, and when we stopped at the window, the girl in the booth almost went into hysterics. "You can't take that thing up there," she said. "Why not," I asked. "It's too big," she exclaimed. "Now I know. I just saw a tour bus going up this hill, and if they can make it, I believe I can too," I said. "You just can't; it's too big," she exclaimed. "I am not any bigger than the bus," I responded. "You just can't, that's why," she declared.

"Can I park in the parking lot here at the Zoo then?" I asked. "Ok," she said finally. We parked in the lot and bought some souvenirs at the little shop at the entrance. We then headed down the hill and back to town. We picked up the trailer and were on our way to Raton, New Mexico.

About fifty miles down the road, I was getting very sleepy. I thought taking my brother-in-law to talk to me was supposed to keep me from this problem. Well, I should have thought longer about this because ol' Bob is not the greatest conversationalist I have ever been with. Bob is a farmer in the upper Panhandle of Texas, and conversation is not one of his strong suits.

I pulled the truck over to the side of the road and told him I couldn't go any further without a little nap time. He said he had been watching me drive, and he thought he could do it for a while. Well heck, he is a farmer and operates machinery and trucks in the harvest.

We were empty, sure, why not? So, I moved to the right side of the big Kenworth cabover in the passenger seat and watched him for about fifteen minutes. He was doing a fairly good job.

"We will be coming to the Raton Pass in about two hours and that should be long enough time for me to sleep. Don't try to go over the pass with me in the sleeper. It is one thing to go down a flat road in one of these things, but to go over the Raton Pass is a whole new ball game," I said.

I crawled into the sleeper, and the next thing I heard was the sound of air brakes coming on. I jumped up and looked out and we were stopping at a stoplight. "Where are we?" I shouted. "In Raton," Bob said, with a grin on his face. "You were sleeping so good I didn't want to wake you, so I went over the pass. This thing ain't so bad once you get the hang of it."

We survived, and I started driving again after we stopped for dinner in Raton. It was now after midnight, and we were in the middle of nowhere, between Raton and Clayton, New Mexico. If you have ever been on this road, you will know what I am saying. There ain't much for eighty or ninety miles.

We were about fifty miles southeast of Raton and we had seen only one car on the road. There were lights of a truck in front of us and we were catching up to this truck very fast. I hit my brakes when I saw the other truck was sitting in the road on the right side, in the middle of the lane, stopped. There was no traffic coming, so I eased over to the left lane and pulled up alongside him.

The truck was an old B-61 Mack, with the engine running and the driver just sitting there looking down the road. "What in the hell is going on," I said to Bob. Bob just looked at me and gave a gesture that indicated he was just as puzzled as I was. I hopped out of my truck, ran around the front, and jumped onto the running boards of the old Mack.

"Something wrong?" I asked. Very slowly, the driver of the Mack turned his head in my direction and said, "Nope, just waiting for the train to go by." I jumped back to the ground and said, "Ok, I just thought you might be having some trouble. See you later." I climbed back into the cab and took off like a shot.

Bob wanted to know what was wrong with the guy. I told him that the driver's eyes looked like dill pickles floating in a bottle of buttermilk. I think he was taking too many "Bennies" or something because he said he was just waiting for the train to go past. "Hell, Bob, there isn't even a train track within twenty miles of here." Well, I can guarantee that was the last time I took one of those little pills ever.

That was also when I decided that making seven hundred dollars a week might not be worth it in the long run. It was also during the same time that I was hoping to make another career change. This change would hopefully find me working in the oil production engineering department of El Paso Natural Gas. I was going to do everything in my power to give up driving the big trucks, at least for a while.

Chapter Sixteen

I made one or more trips hauling cattle, then quit. I went to work hauling groceries, short-haul. Out and in, all on the same day. But first, I took a few days off to go to Farmington, New Mexico, to put in my application with the before-mentioned gas company.

I left for Farmington on June 25th, which is my oldest son's birthday. He was four that morning. I gave him his birthday presents and said goodbye. I put the top down on my new, or almost new, 1969 Olds convertible. It was red with red seats and a blacktop. The weather was warm, and I wanted the air to clear my head of the smell of the cattle truck. I spent three days in New Mexico putting in my application, then went back to driving trucks while the gas company decided when it wanted to hire me. I was confident that they would, but just when was the question.

Around August 15th of the same year, my father bought a new Cadillac and asked me if I wanted to go to Farmington, New Mexico, with him. He told me it was to check out the deer hunting trip for the upcoming fall, but I think it was an excuse for him to drive his new Cadillac on a long trip. It would give me the chance to see if El Paso Natural Gas Co. in Farmington had any intention of hiring me.

The morning after we arrived, I drove my dad's new Cadillac into town to the offices of EPNG. The personnel director's name was Ferdy Ogrin. That is his real name. In my wildest dreams, I couldn't have invented that one. I went up to the receptionist's desk to ask if I could see Mr. Ogrin.

When I walked up to her, she had a small piece of paper in her hand and was dialing a number on the phone. She asked my name, and when I told her what it was, she said, "Excuse me for just a moment," put the phone down and took off down the hall.

I have always been told that most women thought me to be not bad-looking. I had brushed my teeth that morning and didn't think my breath was that offensive. My pants were zipped, and I knew I had removed the strawberry jam from the corners of my mouth after breakfast. For the life of me, I don't know what I said that made her run off like that.

I was about to find out.

In a couple of minutes, she came back, followed by Ferdy Ogrin. He asked me to come into his office, which I did. After proper introductions were completed, Ferdy showed me the small piece of paper the receptionist was holding in her hand when I came in. It had my name, and my phone number in Amarillo, Texas, printed on it.

Ferdy then told me the receptionist was dialing my number when I told her my name. She was calling to ask me if I wanted to go to work for the production engineering department. Well, faster than an anxious groom could answer, I said, "I do." That put me out of the truck driving business for a while, for three and a half years, to be exact.

In the spring of 1975, the production department went on four tens. That meant I would work Monday through Thursday from seven to five. I now had three days off every week. That was fantastic, I now could do all the things around the house I wanted to. I built a garage, a barn, and some corrals and bought twenty Hereford steers. I was going to have it made. I owned five acres in the country, had a nice home, two nice kids, and a wife who hated New Mexico. She was from the Texas Panhandle and wanted to go back there so she could be close to her mommy. I could go into why she was a spoiled brat, but those details would take another complete book.

Well, as I said, this was wonderful, except, after a while, I had built everything I wanted to build and some things that I didn't. We couldn't afford to take a three-day vacation every weekend, so I got bored. I could get a part-time job on the weekends driving a truck. Besides, that year, the cattle market decided to take a plunge, and when I sold the twenty steers, I needed a part-time job. Here we go again.

A friend of mine from work told me about a company in Farmington that hauled gasoline around the state. They were looking for someone to drive part-time so the regular drivers could get a day off. *"This would be perfect,"* I thought. I went to them and told the supervisor I was a truck driver and could work Friday and Saturday for them. He told me they hauled gasoline to stations in Albuquerque, Gallup, and a few other places. "When could you start?" he asked. "This Friday, I get off work Thursday at five," I said.

An extra one hundred per week would be great, and I sure could use it. I found out they only paid twenty-five to thirty-five dollars per load. Well, that's okay, I guess. I can use the fifty or sixty bucks per week as well.

The first Thursday after the meeting, when I returned to the gas company's office at four-thirty in the afternoon, I had a message from the boss at the gasoline transport company. I was to call him when I got in. I did, and sure enough, they had a load for me. The only problem was it was not for Friday morning. They wanted me to pick up a truck and go to Bloomfield, New Mexico and pick up a load of gasoline going to Albuquerque, that night. I called my wife and told her about the load, and to say the least, she was not a happy camper. The longer I was married to her almost everything made her unhappy.

I took the load anyway.

I get into the truck and take off for Bloomfield. I haven't driven in almost four years, and most of that time was what I would call flat land driving. Not too many big hills in the Texas and Oklahoma Panhandles. All of the trucks I have driven had Fuller Road Ranger transmissions in them. Only one gear shift. This truck had a five and four with two gear shifts. I should point out that part of the driving talent I possess is I can drive almost anything and make it look like I have been doing it all my life. Even a truck with two gear shifts in it. I drove with the truck supervisor for a few miles, pulling an empty trailer, and he thought I was very experienced with a five and four. I had all the confidence in my own abilities and was not worried about getting the job done and doing it safely. I would not recommend this to just anyone because you could get killed.

I headed out with the truck and trailer and arrived at Plateau Refinery. They load the truck with over nine thousand gallons of premium gasoline, and I take off for Albuquerque. The highway to Albuquerque is Highway 44. It goes over hills and through an Indian Reservation.

In those days, New Mexico had an open-range law, meaning fences alongside the highway were not as mandatory as they are today. The road was narrow, hilly, rough, tough and had horses, goats, sheep, and the occasional drunk Indian. There was even the Continental Divide to cross, at over seven thousand feet. I get twenty miles south of Bloomfield and the dash lights in the Kenworth conventional go completely out. I can't see the gauges at all, for it has gotten dark.

I pull off the road at a trading post called Nageezi (Navajo) and try to fix it. I try everything I know to no avail. I may be one heck of a driver, but in the fixit department, I lack a few skills. It won't fix. I decide to turn on the dome light on the left side of the cab in hopes I can see the dash. The glare tried to blind me, but at least I could see the dash and gauges. I took a stick of gum from my pocket, put it into my mouth, chewed it up, and then stuck the aluminium wrapper to the lens of the dome light with the gum. It has taken away most of the glare, and there is still enough light to see the dash. I may be a poor mechanic, but that fact has not affected my ability to think fast. I found out later a fuse had blown in the dash. If I had found the new box of fuses that were in the truck, I could have changed it in less than one minute. But hell, this was my first trip in this thing and I had no idea where anything was. The only thing I was worried about was getting the gas out of here before hostiles attacked me and I didn't want to be late on my first load.

I take off again, get over the Continental Divide, and come to the hill that goes into Cuba, New Mexico. This truck does not have a Jake brake, and I know it is very heavy, with nine thousand gallons of gasoline in the tank. I am a little bit nervous about the whole thing. I start off the hill doing all of fifteen to twenty miles an hour. If I were to go off that hill today, I wouldn't even slow down. I would not even think about it. That night, I was thinking about being blown into Texas the fast way.

I finally got the gasoline to its appointed place so it could go into the tanks of cars so they could go down the road killing bugs and burning the gas. I got back to Farmington about nine the next morning. I took the second load of gasoline to Albuquerque that same day as well. By the time I got to the house, the family thought I had gone back on the road for good again.

It was two weeks before I took another load of gasoline on the weekend. When I did, it was to a service station in Gallup, New Mexico. The trip going down there was totally uneventful. On the way back to Farmington, I just about swore off truck driving altogether.

An Indian from a tribe in South Dakota had come to the Four Corners area to hunt for trouble. You see this is because the buffalo have been all but killed off in other books, and this Brave had nothing to hunt in his native land. He must have told his tribe he would go to the land of the Navajo and hunt for big trouble. They didn't declare war on the white man, but they, among other things, made a roadblock on the highway that leads from Gallup to Shiprock.

This is the very road I was on. I don't listen to the radio all that much, and I was totally unprepared for a flock of Native Americans to be in the middle of the road. I was singing Dixie and doing about seventy-five miles per hour when I happened upon this protest group. Being uninformed and in a hurry to get home, I didn't feel I should be a party to this uprising. I didn't even let up on the gas pedal. I guess when they saw the look of surprise in my eyes, and I saw the look of terror in theirs, we mutually agreed to let me pass unharmed. As I went past, the only thing I saw in my mirrors were feathers flying. Hell, I don't know how I missed the one that looked like he was holding a large stick. You don't think that it was a rifle in his hands, do you? I sure hope not because the memory would scare the crap out of me if I thought it was.

My mother told me she heard this renegade's speech that afternoon. Russell Means mentioned some trucker ~~truckers~~ gave them no respect in furthering their cause. If he was the one with the gun, I almost didn't help to further his life either. I don't think I missed him more than two or three inches. I couldn't see all that well because of all the diesel smoke and feathers that were in the air.

I decided to retire from this weekend sport and concentrate on racing motorcycles for I found it to be much safer.

I moved back to Texas in the summer of 1977 and you guessed it, drove a cattle truck again until I bought the closed insurance agency.

On one of these trips, I picked up a load of cows one morning east of Logan, New Mexico going to a feedlot just south of Dalhart, Texas. They were seven hundred-pound heifers. A heifer is a young female cow that has not been bred.

From Interstate 40, I turned east onto US Hwy 60 into Tucumcari, New Mexico. This highway goes through town, and it is four lanes right down Main Street. It was late March and a beautiful Saturday afternoon. As I stopped for a red light in the middle of town, I saw in my mirror a red '59 Ford convertible with four high school girls coming up beside me at the light. I suspect these girls were out riding in Dad's Ford convertible, looking for guys. They were laughing and talking when they pulled up beside me at the light.

Now, one of the young ladies on the second floor of the trailer must not have been impressed by this group of gals in the red Ford. Just before being loaded onto the truck, I think she must have spent considerable time at the feed and water troughs in the corral. Now, just a couple of hours before, these gals were prodded and yelled at to get into the double-deck trailer. Then the thing started moving, and this did not sit well with them at all.

This might be a good time to go into a little more detail on the subject of loading cattle into a double-decker cattle trailer. Well, most of the domestic breeds of cattle are fairly docile critters. To get the friendly bovines to walk nicely onto a loading ramp and get into the trailer, the cowboys, usually not on horseback, will walk behind the herd and shoo them along. Sometimes, this required the help of a contraption known as a cattle prod. This is a fiberglass rod with two prongs at the business end of the prod and batteries at the handle. This prod, when applied to the rear end of a steer, will help them move up the ramp and into the trailer.

This method works well unless the breed of cattle happens to be Santa Gertrudis from south Texas. These bovines have an attitude like another domestic animal known as the Chihuahua. If there were such a thing as a one thousand-pound Chihuahua, they would be worse than Bengal Tigers. Anyway, that South Texas breed of cattle is not friendly at all and will fight anyone on foot with a cattle prod in their hand. I have loaded six or seven loads of this breed and felt lucky to still be alive to write this.

Adding to the cattle's bad attitude and my luck dealing with them back then is the fact that thirty years ago, some of the cattle in feedlots were given a growth hormone known as DES. About two weeks before they were to be shipped to the slaughterhouses, they were taken off of the drug DES. This left the cattle with what is known as withdrawal, which gave the critters almost the same bad attitude as the Santa Gertrudis breed. Once the cowboys get all the heifers or steers in the trailer and get all the gates closed, the driver gets into the truck and then starts driving, which does not sit well with the critters in the trailer either. I sometimes think they heard the cowboys talking about where they would be going, and they really didn't want to go there.

Now, back to the red convertible next to the trailer at the signal light. When the truck stopped at the light and being just a little nervous about the whole situation she found herself in, proved to be more than this heifer could handle. We have all heard the expression shit happens. Well, with her butt up against the side of the trailer and with no warning at all, she let it all go. My guess was about two to three gallons of green residue. From twelve feet in the air, this substance hit the convertible dead center. I have heard screaming before, but not like this. Then there were the hand gestures, some obscene to be sure, as the light turned green. I couldn't help but laugh as I got the big truck moving at a high rate of fuel consumption. A hasty retreat, to say the least. I left the carnage behind and headed for Dalhart, Texas. I would have loved to be watching when these girls got back home and tried to explain to the parents just what and how this happened to them.

I must mention that when I started hauling the cow critters, I was still in high school and had only driven what is called a bobtail truck. No trailer, just the truck. To back one of these things up is about as easy as a car, only longer. These double-decker trailers are forty-eight feet long and with the big diesel trucks total about sixty-five feet in length. That is a whole new ball game.

To get this big rig backed into one of the cattle loading docks, you must be straight and hit the shoot with no gaps between the trailer door and the shoot. If there is a gap of more than three or four inches the cow might get his or her leg in the gap and could cause real damage to the cow's leg.

When Dad bought the first one of these trailers, I had no experience backing one up to a loading dock for cattle. We had just got the big trailer, and on one weekend, Dad asked me if I wanted to go with him and pick up a load of cattle in New Mexico. Sure thing, I told him, and we headed for a ranch just south of Clayton, New Mexico.

When we got to the ranch, I was driving, and Dad said to me, "You want to back into the shoot?" Well as always, I would try anything and said, "Sure do."

About six cowboys were sitting on the corral fence next to the loading dock, waiting for me to get the big rig in the appointed place. I had plenty of room in the pasture so I pulled the big truck about one hundred yards out from the shoot and started backing the thing toward the cattle shoot. Twenty minutes later, with the cowboys on the ground laughing and with Dad's help, I finally got the trailer in the appointed place. When we got back to the house later that evening, I told my mother what an embarrassment that experience was. I also told her it would never happen again. For the next month after school and when I had time, I would practice backing that big truck and trailer to a cattle loading dock. We had one next to the barn at the house and I got to where I could stop the trailer tires on a quarter and no gaps in between it and the shoot. Later in my trucking career, this was a major help to me in some very tight loading and unloading docks.

One of many times this skill was called upon, I had hauled boxed meat from Kansas, T-bones to be exact, to be delivered in Philadelphia, Pennsylvania. The meat distributor was west of downtown, and from the size of the docks, it was not built for the large trucks of today.

Philadelphia has been there for a long time. It was a city when Ben Franklin was there helping to build this country. Well, to make a long story short, I got the trailer backed into the number three dock, and it was not easy. Learning to back a cattle trailer when I was young helped me a lot.

A short time later, a Navajo truck was to unload in dock number one, which was located at the end of the building. Dock number one was at the end of the dock area, next to the offices which extended some fifty feet out from the dock. That caused a small problem because in order to get the trailer into dock number one, you had to back it to the left without hitting the building. The Navajo driver was not able to do this. The poor kid worked for about thirty minutes trying to get the big trailer into dock number one. To add to his woes, it was wintertime and starting to spit snow a little bit. The driver opened the door to the cab of his truck and he was sweating like it was ninety degrees outside.

I walked out to his truck and asked him if he would like some help backing this rig into the dock. He finally said okay, and I climbed into the cab and backed the trailer into the dock on the first try. The Navajo driver just stood there in the middle of the parking lot, shaking his head. When I climbed out of the cab, he asked me how I did that so easily. I then told him about hauling a lot of cattle when I was younger and into some crazy places. I told him you just need a lot more practice and you will be fine.

Chapter Seventeen

Yep, driving a truck can be a very interesting profession. It is amazing to see the many different types of people who have followed this career path. I'm not even taken by surprise anymore when I meet a fellow trucker (male or female) who has been an ex-teacher, ex-banker, ex-engineer, or who carries a bona fide PhD in their back pocket.

In this day of fast-paced living, people are searching for something better, something more rewarding, and something that will fulfill the inner need for adventure. All of us need some adventure in our lives, or we might end up in the looney bin twiddling our thumbs and humming to ourselves for the rest of our days. And trucking can meet this need.

My dad drove a truck in the late 1930's hauling cotton from Southwestern Oklahoma to Houston Texas, and dad told me a few of the stories of his travels out on the road. He also taught me how to drive and to drive well.

φ

Dad was in the Quartermaster core in the army after spending almost three years as a drill sergeant for basic training. In France and Germany in 1945, they trucked supplies from the coast of France to the front lines. When Dad came home in November of 1945, he would tell his family some of his stories from the war.

This is the mystery and suspense part of the book. I have been told that all good books need to have some mystery and suspense in them. So here goes. One such story was when my father was stationed in Durham, North Carolina.

He got a weekend pass and was walking down the street in the downtown area when a girl in a Buick convertible stopped next to him and asked if my dad would help her with a problem. He said he would help and got into the Buick with the woman.

They drove only about two blocks from where she picked him up and parked in front of an apartment building. The woman was very good-looking and told him she lived on the second floor. "Come on with me," she said.

They climbed the stairs, and when they got to the woman's apartment, she took a key from her purse and unlocked the door. Once inside, the lady said, "I'll fix us a drink, so make yourself comfortable."

Dad was wearing one of those army caps that had no bill and was narrow at the top. He took his cap off and tossed it onto the arm of the couch that was across the living room. The cap fell off the arm of the couch and fell to the floor next to it. He quickly went to pick up the cap, and when he leaned over to get it, he noticed there was a man's arm he could see behind the couch.

He looked toward the kitchen where the lady was fixing the drinks and said, "Listen honey, I am a married man, and my wife is on her way to North Carolina with my five-month-old son. I think I should be going now because I think this could get out of hand." The woman walked over to Dad, put her arm on his shoulder, and kissed him on the cheek.

The family who was listening to this story in the living room of Granny West's home was a large group. Dad had four brothers and three sisters. Two of his brothers were there with their wives, and one of his sisters and her husband. These folks were farmers in rural southwestern Oklahoma. This was in 1945 and there was no television to get all the news of the war. What little news they got was from the newspapers and the radio.

These folks had never been out of Oklahoma or Texas, and getting a story about the war put everyone on the edge of their seats, taking in every word. Well, Dad went on with the story.

The woman then said, "You saw what was behind the couch," and reached her hand into the pocket of her sweater. She quickly pulled a shiny pistol from her pocket and pointed it at Dad. "Do you really think I got you up here to make love to you? I need your help getting rid of the guy who is behind the couch," she said. She continued, "So take hold of the arm and pull him out from there." Looking down the barrel of a .38 and thinking she was the one who put the guy behind there, he thought he had better do as she wanted.

He took hold of the man's arm and pulled him from behind the couch. There was a hole with some blood around it in the middle of the man's chest and his white dress shirt. He saw that the man was dead and asked the woman, "What do we do now?" She told him, "We will put him in my car." He then asked her, "Then what?" "We will take him to the country and bury him," she said.

Dad was getting very nervous by that time. He noticed the dead man was shot only one time, and from the hole in his shirt, she was a good shot. The bullet appeared to have gone through his heart.

Then Dad said, "Let's pick up this guy and get him in between us and walk him down to your car." She replied that would be good so anyone who saw them would think the guy was drunk and would not get alarmed.

So, they picked the dead guy up, put his arms around their shoulders, and went out the door of the woman's apartment. The hallway was not well-lit. As they started toward the stairs, a man was coming up the stairs, and when he got to the hallway asked them, "You guys got a drunk?"

The woman answered, "Sure do. He had way too much to drink, and we are taking him out to get some fresh air." The man then asked, "What is that on his shirt?" and came closer to get a better look.

With a look of shock on his face, the man then said, "That's a bullet hole in his shirt, and I think he is dead." He then quickly turned toward the other end of the hallway, where there was a payphone on the wall.

Dad whispered to the woman, "I'll take care of this; hold this guy up," and he turned loose of the dead guy. They propped him against the wall, and Dad started toward the man, going to the phone. He said, "I grabbed the fellow by the shoulder, and when I hit him, I hit the bedpost and woke myself up."

By that time in the story, all of Dad's family was sitting on the edge of their seats, and when he said the punch line, they went wild. One of Dad's brothers and one of his brothers-in-law got so mad they wanted to fight. When they all came to their senses, they laughed about it and said it was one hell of a story they didn't expect. Then Dad told them, "I will tell you guys a real war story."

And so, he did. He told them three weeks before the end of the war, he was leading a convoy of six trucks in his Jeep. They were taking supplies to the front lines when they saw two German fighter planes coming from the north. When the planes got close enough to be seen really well, the planes did not have propellers on the front. These were the new German jet fighters.

Not one of dad's family knew what these things were. They had read about it some in the papers, but that was it. He told them Germany did have these new types of planes. The jet fighters actually shot at him and his men while they were in their trucks. He told them the jets made only one pass and didn't hit any of the trucks in the convoy.

He continued with his story. That night about two in the morning, he heard a noise in the warehouse, where he was sleeping like he did every night. He grabbed his carbine and went to check out the noise.

In the middle of the warehouse floor was Ott Wallas, who was also from Fredrick, Oklahoma. He asked Ott what he was doing here at two in the morning. He had .50 caliber machine gun belts everywhere on the floor. Ott told him he was making a machine gun belt with nothing but tracer bullets. A tracer bullet has phosphorus in the bullet, so when it is fired, it leaves a trail of fire. Hence, the name tracer because you can see where it is going.

Ott went on to explain the German fighter planes have rubber gas tanks in their wings. If a tracer bullet hits one of the gas tanks, it will catch it on fire. Ott told me he was going to shoot down a German fighter plane using these bullets. He planned to fire the tracers at the gas tanks and catch their wings on fire. I told Ott to hurry up, finish, and get some sleep. The convoy was going back into Germany the next day with more supplies.

The next day, around noon, they were headed toward Germany with six or seven trucks of supplies. He said it was a beautiful day in Germany: few clouds, blue skies, and a nice drive to the front lines.

From the rear of the trucks, they could hear a plane coming at them, a Messerschmitt ME 109 fighter plane. The convoy stopped and the plane fired only two or three rounds at them and then quit. Then he flew right over the tops of the trucks from about 100 feet up without a shot.

Ott had his chance and didn't waste it. He opened fire with the 50-caliber machine gun, which was mounted on the back of the Jeep. Both wings of the German fighter plane caught on fire. The plane turned skyward, and at about two thousand feet, the pilot bailed out of the plane. He came down only about one-half-mile from them on the same road.

He told the truck drivers to stay right where they were. He and Ott would be back in a while. They drove to where the pilot came down and saw him sitting on a rock next to the road. He had his hands in the air when the Jeep got to where he was sitting.

The first thing the German fighter pilot said to them was, "Hello fellows, how are you doing this fine day?" Dad then told everyone that the German spoke perfect English, with almost no accent at all.

Ott Wallas had the .50-caliber machine gun pointed at the German fighter pilot. The guy was smiling at us and then said, "Well, I guess the war is over for me." He told us he was out of ammo, and he didn't even know if he had enough fuel to get back to the airbase. Then he gave me his German Lugar pistol and got into the Jeep.

I asked him how did he speak English so well? The pilot told us he had gone to the University of Chicago and graduated in 1939. He went back to Germany when the war started. He told us he was drafted into the air-core as a fighter pilot. He also said he was not in favor of Hitler or the war, but he had no option but to do as he was told. He then said, "May I ask a question?" I told him, sure, go ahead. The pilot then asked. "How are the Cubs doing this year?" I then looked at Ott Wallas and, with a funny grin, said, "Terrible as always."

Chapter Eighteen

What other profession can offer you so much adventure? On the West Coast today and on the East Coast tomorrow. You can find yourself in the middle of an earthquake on Sunday and in a huge snowstorm on Monday. I was actually in an earthquake in Ontario, California.

I had just parked the truck at the TA Truck Stop in Ontario and went into the café for some nourishment. A couple of other buddy truckers I had met were sitting at a booth, and I joined them. After ordering iced tea, we started conversing about the loads we were getting or not getting, as the case was that day. The waitress returned to our booth and set the iced tea glass in front of me on the table. And bang, it hit!

I reached for my tea, and the darn glass came up to meet me! I first thought someone had kicked the table. I looked up at the waitress and saw sheer fright. The guys I was with were looking at the ceiling, so I looked up too. The steel girders were actually waving like spaghetti noodles. The next thing I knew, we were all standing outside of the building, and the waitress was next to me, still holding her tray and the rest of the iced tea.

We moved so fast. How we got out of the building is still a blur today. I turned to look at the trucks parked in the lot and saw trailers swaying, almost touching each other at their tops.

After it all settled down, we promptly went back into the café. Now, this truck stop in Ontario is huge, with a deli, café, barbershop, showers, laundries, convenience store, and even a movie theatre. Everything was still intact, and we all went back to doing exactly what we were doing before the quake hit. Now I know why they call this place "Shaky Town."

Being on the road can increase your vocabulary three-fold. And if you have a three-fold vocabulary already, you can have fun bewildering the heck out of some people you meet.

One day in February 1990, I stopped at a truck stop in Portland, Oregon.

It was the evening of the heavyweight championship fight between Mike Tyson and Buster Douglas. When I walked into the area where truckers pay for their fuel, all the talk was about the fight. The girl behind the counter was giving a blow-by-blow account of the final round to four or five truckers.

"Buster hit him with a right hand that sent the champ to the canvas, and the ref stopped the fight with Buster Douglas, the winner." Her arms were swinging wildly with her vivid description of the knockout. I, being very surprised at the outcome of the fight, said, "You don't mean that Buster Douglas has knocked out Mike Tyson?"

With this statement, she went into a swinging of her arms again and repeated the fight's end. I then looked her right in the eyes and said "Well, I guess that caused a medicery felum resulting in the delinkwishes of his enamorada. With a slightly bewildered look on her face she exclaimed, "You're darn right it did, and he didn't get up after that." Everyone in the room now had a bewildered look. Smiling, I calmly walked back to my truck and went on my way.

In the trucking business you can have more fun than a barrel of monkeys. But remember, it's not all fun and games. Ridiculous deadlines, the inevitable "call me back in an hour program" after you just practically killed yourself getting to point A, and the loneliness of being on the road by yourself.

When I'm on the road, my phone bill almost triples, and I'm sure Ma Bell doesn't mind. In fact, they have even called to find out if there's a problem when my phone bill falls below $300 a month. "No, nothing's wrong, but I'll be, as Willey sings it, "On the road again, maybe one of these days," I tell them.

Chapter Nineteen

Enough harking back on my truck driving career and back to my move to Las Vegas, Nevada. The trucking school was closed during the Christmas week until after the New Year. I was to graduate from the dealers' school the following week. I had auditioned at a casino in Henderson and they told me I would have a job when I got back from Albuquerque, New Mexico. I had told them my father was very sick with cancer and I wanted to go see him.

I got back from New Mexico and graduated from the dealers' school the first week of January, 1993. I was to start work at the Henderson casino the next Monday. But on Friday, my mother called me and said that my father had just passed away. The funeral was to be in Spearman, Texas, the next week. I told her we would be there. I then called the casino and told them about my father. They said they could not hold the job for another week. I told them that would be okay with me, although it really wasn't.

I could and then couldn't understand their attitude, but there was nothing that would stop me from going to my father's funeral.

We went to Spearman, Texas, the next week, and when I got back to Las Vegas, I started looking for a casino that would hire a break-in dealer.

I also went to the driver's school and told them I was leaving because I was going to work for a casino. They did not want me to quit and offered me more money if I stayed. I told them that I was sorry, but I had gone to dealers' school, and I wanted to give it a try. They wished me well and good luck. I

165

would soon learn that good luck was something I would say to tens of thousands of people in the next few years. In fact, hundreds of thousands of people because I stayed as a dealer in casinos for the next fifteen years.

My last dealing job was at Wynn Las Vegas. It was one of the highest-paying dealing jobs in the industry, paying in the six-figure range. I would still be there, but I finally had to retire because of a spine injury that I was told would only get worse the longer I stood as a blackjack dealer.

When I got back from Texas after my dad's funeral and needed to find another dealing job, I went to a new small casino that was about to open in Henderson. I applied and got a job dealing blackjack.

On the opening night of the casino, the casino manager asked me if I could deal ~~with~~ roulette. I told him I learned it in dealers' school, but as this is my first dealing job, I haven't dealt on a live game. "No problem," he said. I thought to myself, *"This is going to be a fun night with some of the Boyd Group here."* Well, it was a little more than just a few of the big boys; they were all there.

The first group that sat down at the roulette wheel was none other than Sam Boyd Jr. His wife and son were also there. The Boyd Group owned Sam's Town and four other casinos in Vegas. I had fun, and these were just nice folks.

The next day I dealt blackjack all day. About five in the afternoon, five guys came over to my table, which was empty. They were Hell's Angels from Nevada. The pit boss looked nervous, to say the least. These guys were very polite and about as nice as they could be. We had a great time for the hour I dealt to them. And there were no problems at all. The pit boss calmed down quite a bit.

At the end of the first month, they laid off some of the dealers. It is a pattern with casinos because when a new place opens, they all hire too many dealers. I was one of those who got the ax. I went the next day down to Fremont Street and applied at the Golden Gate Casino, which is one of the oldest casinos in Vegas. To this day, it is still known as a break-in house because they will hire new dealers fresh out of school.

I started the next day on the ten-to-six schedule, also known as the day shift. This is where I really learned to deal blackjack. The casino was always busy, and it was a good dealing job, but not much money. I stayed there only a couple of months and found a job at the Lady Luck Casino. This was much better pay for a small place downtown. I stayed there for about a year and a half. I started on the graveyard shift.

After about a month of being at Lady Luck, I wanted to sell a weight-lifting machine that I didn't have room for at the apartment my wife and I had rented. I put a note on the bulletin board in the dealers' breakroom. The next day, the casino manager asked me what I wanted for the machine. I told him seven hundred dollars, or two hundred fifty dollars, and a day shift job. The next day, I started on days. That's how it works in Vegas, as well as most other places in this world.

One day at the Lady Luck, I had a couple sit down at my table to play some blackjack. This gal had tattoos on her cheeks of a skull and crossbones. She got up to go to the potty room, and I asked the fellow where they were from. "Haiti," he said, "and my wife is a Voodoo Priestess." My next thought was, dear, *God let her win so she doesn't make one of those little dolls and start sticking pins in it.* They didn't lose, and I was spared the agony of dying a slow death.

Another time, I was at a dead table when a fellow sat down at the table next to mine. As I had no one to deal to I watched what was going on while protecting my table. He played five one hundred dollar bills the first hand. Now, this was a six-deck shoe game, and when the dealer got to the shuffle, the guy had won $103,500 and left. He did not lose a single hand and had only three pushes. Wow, I thought, this could only happen once in a thousand times or more. The major problem was that he came back the next weekend and thought he could do it again. He ended up losing $35,000, and we never saw him again after that. One can have incredible luck sometimes, but it cannot be repeated often in a casino in Vegas.

We got a new casino manager a few months later and he decided we should have new dealer shirts. The shirts he decided on were red and yellow and made from a material that was close to a raincoat. It was late spring in Vegas, and the outside temperature was reaching the one-hundred mark. When I would leave the casino to go to my car in the shirt, I would sweat like crazy.

A new casino had just opened, only one mile from my house, called the Boulder Station. I wanted to check them out to see what kind of clientele they had, if the dealers were making any money, and how much. I knew one of the pit bosses there so I went to talk to him one evening. He told me I should come here and go to work as a dealer. He said, "We could use someone as good as you have become."

A few days later, I went to Boulder Station and auditioned for a dealer's job. When I was asked if I could deal with Roulette, I said "yes," and the casino manager put me on a left-handed Roulette table with no players. He said he would be the player and he put up a bet that was not a normal one.

I had never seen a left-handed table before. Not wanting to look like I could not deal a left-handed table, I just spun the ball like I had done it for years. Success, the little ball dropped into a number, and I was able to fool the casino manager. And maybe it was because, in my earlier life, I had broken my right arm twice and had to become left-handed for a while. I became so good at being a lefty that it was no problem. I paid the bet off with only one hand just like the book said I was to do. This must have impressed the manager so much that he then said can you start tomorrow night on the swing shift. "Yes, sir," I said, "and what time would you like me to be here?" "Seven p.m. to three a.m. is the swing shift here," he explained. I told him I would be here to start, and he took me to get all the paperwork done.

Now, I just needed to go to the Lady Luck Casino and tell them that I was quitting. In Las Vegas casinos, there was very little thought or actually giving of a two-week notice to quit your job as a dealer. In the casino business, your income is based on minimum wage plus tips. If the House you were dealing in didn't have good tipping clientele, dealers would move on in the blink of an eye to another place to make more tip money. One cannot live on minimum wage alone.

When I left Lady Luck, they asked me to put three reasons I was quitting on their exit sheet, and I put Ugly Shirts, not enough money, and Ugly Shirts. It was the truth.

On to Boulder Station on swing shift. It was more money, and the casino was new, which meant a lot of customers. I started dealing Roulette my first night there on the roulette table where you spun the ball with your left hand. During the audition, I looked like I had been dealing it for years. Well things don't always go the right way when it's your first night dealing the game for real.

One of the first players who sat down at the Roulette wheel was a lady with a magnificent cleavage showing. The first time I spun the ball while she was playing, the little ball wound up; guess where. Yep, right between the hooters and into the scanty garment she was wearing. No, I didn't retrieve the little ball myself. The second time I spun the ball, it took off and landed in the coin return of a slot machine, which was located just behind the gal. I was glad the casino manager was not down on the casino floor that evening. The pit boss walked over to me and said, "I'll bet you can't spin the ball into her blouse again." "Should I try?" I asked. He was laughing so hard I didn't quite understand his reply.

One Saturday night, I had a fellow playing blackjack, and he was the only one at the table. This guy was about thirty-five years old and wearing a brown leather jacket. He was almost bald but a nice-looking fellow. The game was a double-deck pitch blackjack game. He was trying to catch the cards in the air before they hit the table! Now this takes hand speed way out of the ordinary. Saying this guy had fast-hand speed would be a gross understatement. After a few hands, he put up a bet of twenty-five dollars in chips. I was determined to deal the cards fast enough so this fellow could not catch the card in the air. The first card hit the stack of twenty chips, went through the stack, and made two stacks of ten chips each. The pit boss was watching the game and said: "who wants a side bet as to whether the dealer could do that trick again." We laughed and I then asked the player what he did for a living.

He turned to the right slightly so I could see his right shoulder. The jacket had a round patch that read Universal Studios Stunt Department. I said, "So you are a stuntman." He said, "Yes. I have made my living jumping out the windows of three-story buildings for fifteen years. If I had your hair, I would have been Tom Cruise." I did and still do have the TV evangelist hair. Now, it is mostly gray, but thank God, I still have it all.

When I was at the Boulder Station Casino, I was still using some stuff called Just for Men to keep the color my natural brown. A couple of years later, after stopping the use of the hair dye, my hair turned mostly grey. A lady walked up to a blackjack table I had just opened and gave me a one-hundred-dollar chip for a tip. She told me that I had the most beautiful hair she had ever seen.

She didn't even sit down and play she just kept on walking through the casino. After about a year at Boulder Station, I was getting tired of getting off work at three in the morning. My wife was working a 9 a.m. to 5 p.m. job so I would have coffee with her before she left for work and just had barely enough time in the evening to visit with her about her day. I slept while she worked, and she slept while I worked.

So, I moved on to a couple of other casinos to get a day job. I worked for the San Remo and The Texas Station for about half of a year and decided I wanted to go back downtown.

The four months I worked for San Remo were not very productive. The money we made was worse than Lady Luck. The San Remo was behind the Tropicana Hotel, just off the strip.

It was a small casino with only about two hundred rooms. I thought because of the location it should be alright for dealers' tips—wrong. One Saturday, I was on a blackjack game for eight hours and did not deal a card. The only saving grace for the place was it was very friendly, and I got to deal craps. I had learned the game in dealers' school, but never did deal the game in a casino. The casino manager asked me if I knew the game and I told him yes. He said, "Well, you need to deal, so you go on the game after your next break." *"Well, this was going to be interesting,"* I thought and hoped.

The first few days were fun, and I was learning to deal craps. *"The more you know in Vegas, the better,"* I thought. One day a player walked over to the craps table at my end and just stood back and watched for a couple of rolls. I had never seen this guy before, and when he moved up to the table, he just stood there as the stick man was about to move the dice. He then threw five hundred dollars in twenties on the table and started

171

calling off bets. There were about six bets, he called out, and I just looked over at him and said, "What!!"

The pit boss fell to the floor laughing. He finally got up off the floor and, still laughing, said, "That was the best call I have ever seen." The stick man pushed all the money back to the player and said, "Next roll." Well, the player went ballistic, grabbed all the money, and went to another table. I asked the pit boss if I had done something wrong.

Now, as this player walked to the next table, I could see the jacket he was wearing. The jacket had a picture of him on the back with these words, "You Think You're Lucky—You're Watching I'm Playing!"

I asked, "Who is that guy?" The pit boss told me his family once owned Caesars Palace. "The San Remo is about the only casino in Vegas that will let him play because of the way he does things like you just saw."

"Did I do something wrong with what I did?" I asked. The pit boss then said, "That was the funniest thing I have seen in a long time, and no, you did nothing wrong." I will not mention this fellow's name because he is also an attorney from Los Angeles, California.

On to Texas Station Casino, where I worked after their opening for about a month, and that was long enough. Station Casinos is a large company that owns about five local-styled casinos in Las Vegas. It is a family-owned company. One small problem they have or had is hiring old buddies into big jobs in some of their places. I know of two or three big boo-boos in management while I was in the business.

Texas Station hired a friend as the casino manager who was supposed to know what he was doing. This fellow's name was Robin Hood; yes, really, it was Robin Hood. I didn't even know the Robin Hood of old, even though I am old but I'm not

On The Right Side of The Road ~ Tom West

that old. Well, this name's sake should have been running from the Sheriff of Nottingham instead of trying to run a casino. By the end of the first week, after we were opened, he had changed the shuffle on blackjack seven times. There was no second week, for he was fired at the end of the first week. Once again, a new casino over-hires for their grand opening so I only lasted one month there.

I auditioned at the Four Queens, and they hired me for the day shift. On the first day on the job, the casino manager asked if I knew craps. "Yes," I said. "I have dealt craps at the San Remo for a short period of time." He said that would be alright and told me I would sit box on one of their craps tables today. Sure, I told him and asked, "Which table?" and he told me table number three. Boy, was I going to get a lesson in craps that day!

The four dealers were from England and each of them had been casino managers in Africa. These guys could really deal the craps game like no one I had ever seen. I just sat there in amazement most of the day. At the Four Queens, the craps pit was table-for-table on the tips sharing. I knew some of the casinos on the strip were table for table, but it was a surprise to find the Four Queens did that as well. Now, as I said, these guys could really deal. I saw moves that were not in any dealers' book for casinos in Vegas. I honestly had no idea what they were doing most of the time.

At the end of the day, each of the dealers on that table made over one thousand dollars each. They each gave me twenty-five dollars, which was over and above the casino's pay for a box man. The box man didn't share in the table tips. I think they also paid the pit boss over two hundred dollars that day, who also didn't share in the table tips. I have no idea whether these dealers were not honest, but this would make them about the highest-paid dealers in Las Vegas. I also did not know how long the table-for-table tip sharing had been going on at the

173

Four Queens, but as luck would have it, things were about to change.

When I came to work the next day, I heard the new general manager had fired the casino manager along with all the craps crews. And that the craps tables would no longer be table-for- table tips. Well, at least I got to see this type of stuff one time.

Dealing at the Four Queens went just fine for about a year, and then, one day, a new lady dealer was hired. Camille was about twenty-five and very good-looking. Within the first week, she was there, she filed a complaint against one of the pit bosses for, as it was stated, making unwanted advances toward her. Well, I thought this would be possible in Vegas or anywhere else for that matter. It was the talk of the breakroom for all the next week.

Camille was on the same break as me the next week, and one of those days, I asked her where she was from. This was the wrong thing to ask her. As it would turn out, asking this gal anything was the wrong thing to do. She went into a rage and wanted to know why I would ask her where she was from. "Just asking," I said, "just making conversation."

She said, "I am from Tijuana, Mexico." Then I made really bad mistake by saying, "Wow, you don't even have any accent at all." She said, "What do you think I am, a Mexican whore?" I could not believe what she just said back to me. I was going to apologize to her when she went off the deep end and started calling me everything she could think of. The twenty-minute break was over, and I went back to the blackjack table. I was wondering what was wrong with this dealer.

I was to find out later that day.

Two breaks later, the pit boss told me that the casino manager wanted to see me when I went on break. I went to his office, and the casino manager had a funny grin on his face. He told me Camille had filed a complaint against me for harassment. Really, I told him. He said something is not on the up and up with this dealer, Camille. He told me not to worry about the complaint he would throw it in the trash. He said just stay far away from her from now on. "Sure," I said, "no problem. I'm not sure what her problem is, but she has one."

The next day, I was in the breakroom, and in came Camille. She walked right over to where I was sitting and started calling me everything but a white man. Then she stomped out of the breakroom in a huff. I had not said anything to her, and everyone in the breakroom was laughing and saying, "What did you do to her."

"Nothing that I know of. I think she is just a little looney or something," I responded. Then I did a bad thing: I saw one of the little brooms that the maintenance people use in casinos. I took the little broom and put it through the lock on Camille's locker. I went back on the game, and at the next break, the pit boss told me the casino manager wanted to see me.

The manager asked me if I had put a broom into the lock on Camille's locker. "Yes, I did because from all she said to me, I figured she was a witch, and I wanted to give her a new car to drive," I responded.

The manager then said, "I should write you up for that, but I won't do it." I told the manager, "Oh, go ahead because I will be the only dealer who has ever been written up for brooming a dealer, and I want to put the write-up, framed, on my wall at my house." We were both laughing, and he gave me the paper.

That same week, Camille was fired. The casino manager had called some of the casinos Camille had worked at before coming to the Four Queens. He found out she had filed complaints against pit bosses and dealers at every place she had worked in the last year. I guess she had a real problem.

A few months later, I heard that the Golden Nugget was hiring dealers. I applied and got a job dealing there. I stayed at the Golden Nugget for almost eight years. The money I made there was much more than anywhere I had worked; in fact, by over $20,000 per year. This was a very good dealing job for downtown Las Vegas.

I met many celebrities at the Golden Nugget. There were pro Golfers, people in the entertainment business, and many more notables during my eight years there.

One day, I opened up a blackjack game in pit five, and the pit boss was a fellow who had been in the casino business for many years. He had worked for all the strip casinos during the mafia days. He wasn't really happy with the changes that had been made after the mafia was kicked out of the casino industry in the mid-1980s. He was old school and walked over to me when I got the table opened.

Tony asked me if I knew what a clerk dealer was. I said, "Yes, I read what it means when I went to dealers' school." It is the best of the best, the dealers' dealer. One who very rarely makes mistakes protects the table and the money at it and deals the cards without a hitch.

Tony then said, "I have never really liked you because you are a showboat." He then said, "But if there ever was a dealer who should be called a clerk, it is you. You never make a mistake, and most dealers make two or three mistakes every hour."

I said, "Thank you for the compliment." I was actually shocked because to be called a clerk dealer is a very high honor in the casino business.

Then Tony said, "You're welcome, and I still don't like you because you are still a showboat." He just smiled and walked away. After that, he never said much to me but would just smile and watch the other dealers in the pit.

In 2005, Steve Wynn opened the Wynn Las Vegas, and it was the most expensive hotel ever built at four and one half-billion dollars. It was built on the site of the old Desert Inn. I thought I would be too old to even put in an application there. Then I got a call from the casino manager, and he asked me to come and see him.

I did and he asked me if I wanted to be a pit boss at the new casino, which wasn't opened yet. I said, "Well if you are offering me a job, I would like to just be a blackjack dealer there."

"Okay," he said. He added, "Do the paperwork, and you will start when we open in about three weeks."

Well, I thought, this is going to be a big change for me. This would be the highest-paying dealing job in Vegas. Wow, the big time after only thirteen years in the business. It was a six-figure dealing job the first year despite the five weeks I took off during the year.

In my second year at Wynn, I was asked to go to Macau, China, and supervise the opening of the new Wynn Macau. Our job was to train the floor supervisors on what to look for to keep the casino out of trouble with the regulating agency for gaming in their country. We watched the dealers, and if we recognized a problem, we would take it up with the floor supervisor or pit boss. It was their job to tell the dealer and correct the error or the dealer. We did not deal any of the games because we weren't licensed there to do that.

Getting ready for the trip and my new responsibilities, I thought that this was going to be one heck of a trip. It definitely was.

We flew to China in a mere fourteen hours. The worst part was knowing I had to fly back in the same amount of time, and I was dreading that. Sitting on an airplane for that long is painful, to say the least.

We got to Macau, and boy, did I learn a lot in the next month. They had told us about half of the people could speak some English. As we were to find out, maybe one in one hundred could even say more than yes or no in English. I was also to learn that in this part of China, very little rice is served in any place you would eat. It was noodles and more noodles. It was also during the bird flu epidemic time in China and all food was cooked to the consistency of a Lay's Potato Chip. This over-cooking of everything, along with the inevitable diet of noodles that was their mainstay in China, proved to be better than joining Weight Watchers. I thought I was going to starve to death until we found a Pizza Hut and a McDonalds in the Sands Hotel. The last two weeks we were there we ate at the Pizza Hut every other night. I thought when I got home, my wife would not know me. I would be just so skinny; she would think I had been sick the whole time I was over there.

While I was at the Golden Nugget, I dealt to a lot of people, many famous movie and TV folks, and a lot of sports folks as well. One day, I had an almost full table of players. The only empty seat was in the middle of the table, right in front of me. This young man sat down, and the first hand I dealt from the double deck, he put both hands on the cards. I very politely said, "You may not hold the cards with both hands. This is because there are people in this world that if they get both hands on the cards, the ten and four you are holding would turn into an ace and jack." He then said, "I don't believe in magic."

The fellow at the end of the table, who was wearing a short-sleeve shirt, said to him, "So you don't believe in magic." The guy in the middle responded, "No, I don't." Then, the fellow at the end of the table asked the guy, "Do you smoke?" The answer was yes. The end of the table fellow then said, "Let me give you a cigarette," and held out his hand to the middle of the table. His hand was not more than a foot in front of my face. He closed his fist and then opened it with a filter cigarette in the middle of his hand. The guy in the middle of the table, with a look of surprise, took the smoke from his hand. Without moving his hand, the fellow who produced the cigarette then said, "Let me light it for you." He closed his fist again and pointed at the cigarette with his index finger while holding his thumb back. When his thumb closed into his hand below his index finger, a flame about two inches long came from the finger. He lit the cigarette and blew out the fire on the end of his finger.

Now, all this time, his hand was not more than a foot from my face. I didn't see any wires, no nothing to produce a cigarette and a flame. Everyone at the table had their mouths open in awe of this trick. The fellow then took a business card from his shirt pocket and dropped it on the table. The card had his name on it, identifying that he was from Paris, France and that he was the World Champion Hand Magician. I showed everyone at the table this man's business card.

This was just a small sample of the things I saw in fifteen years as a dealer in the casinos of Las Vegas. As a matter of fact, I could write another entire book on the things I saw but I know many others have probably done that already and done it very well.

About one year after going to China, I got a severe back problem, and a doctor in Reno, Nevada, told me I should seriously think about retiring. So, I did.

Chapter Twenty

Before going to Las Vegas, I decided to finish writing down my memories of driving a truck before I moved into another career. So, I've been busy writing this literary piece, so all who have wondered about the trucking business can get a quick glimpse of what does and can happen on the road. Interesting, huh?

And these events all happened before my casino career which started in 1992!

You might also wonder how a guy can go from farmer, oilman, banker, truck driver to casino dealer. Well, let me explain. It has always been known that you only get one chance at life. There is no book of instructions on how to live that life. My mother once said she wished there was a book of instructions that came with each child. Then she would say it probably would only fit one person. All the rest would be on their own.

When I was a kid, and roamed the canyons north of Borger, Texas, whenever we could, it was for the adventure. There was never any fear of what we might find out there. It was just for the adventure of it. I grew up looking for this type of adventure. Life can be like that if your head is on straight. When I went to Las Vegas with my dad in 1972, the first person I met was the movie star Groucho Marx. I knew Las Vegas would be another adventure and a good one. I never had a fear of the unknown, as most people I have met do.

There's an old saying that you have nothing to fear except fear itself. This saying I have found to be true for the most part. I have also said many times that Columbus took a chance, so why shouldn't I?

This way of thinking could get a person in trouble if they are not careful and at least have some idea of what they are getting into. I might have been lucky sometimes, but I don't really believe in luck all that much. I have always had a desire to succeed in almost everything I have done in life, so I tried to do just that.

But back to truck driving and my career in that profession. As a truck driver, you have a great deal of responsibility. The rig you are driving is worth between $125,000 to $150,000 if you drive for a trucking company. The load you are carrying could be worth anywhere from $30,000 to $1,000,000 or more. Making sure the equipment is working as it should be is another responsibility. As the professional driver out on the highways and byways, you need to contend with all the other drivers who are herding their vehicles down the road, which could be a chore all in itself.

I do admit that driving a truck is surely not for everyone, but to those who might feel inclined to give it a try, go ahead. It can be a rewarding vocation. It will pay more money than the national averages and as you have learned, it can have some interesting events. You will get to see a lot more of the United States than you will if you work in a store. You will meet some interesting folks out there, and if you are good at it, it will be good for you.

As I write this, I must confess I haven't been trucking in a few years now.

But who knows, I might be back out there and our paths just might cross somewhere down the road. I have retired from working in the mainstream. I have not retired from life and adventure. At seventy-five years old, I have not slowed down much. I do some things a little slower than I once did, but not much. I was told by many that I had not lived a normal life. Well, if that is true, then I usually ask them, what is normal?

If you are out there right now, remember to always keep the shiny side up and the dirty side down. But above all, always remember that in this country, it is better to drive ON THE RIGHT SIDE OF THE ROAD!

Epilogue

I am writing this update to the Epilogue in February 2025 as a fitting ending to the stories I have written in this book about driving over-the-road trucks. Although most of this book was written in 1990 from my personal experience driving the big rigs, it was finished early in the year 2025.

The truckers of this country most definitely deserve our heartfelt gratitude for what these brave men and women who drive the big rigs are doing. They deliver everything needed by our country - from our food and essential supplies to stores nationwide to delivering the much-needed medical supplies to hospitals and health care facilities everywhere.

Throughout the years, the over-the-road truckers, of which there are over 8.5 million, combined with the nearly 3 million short-haul drivers, have delivered everything we use each and every day, no matter what challenges they may face daily while on the road. They are an integral part of our country, and, in my opinion, it is a great profession to be in.

So, thank you for all you do for our great country. I hope this book brings a smile to your face and some laughter at what we, the truck drivers, experience every day as we are "On The Right Side Of The Road." Stay safe out there....

About the Author

Tom West lives in east central Oklahoma. He retired from the casino business in 2007. After 20 years of living in the fast lane in Las Vegas, Nevada, he calls the country his home and thoroughly enjoys it.

After Tom finished writing his autobiography, "The Most Interesting Man You Have Never Met," he was encouraged to continue writing by Dr. A. W. Sibley, a published author himself, and numerous others. He recalled writing, over thirty years ago, about his experiences as a truck driver from a diary he had kept. By chance, Tom checked the briefcase he used while trucking, and the printed manuscript was inside. The manuscript was edited and expanded to include more stories about his trucking career, which started back in high school. Tom also added a few more events from his life over the past 75 years, and "On The Right Side Of The Road" was resurrected from the archives.

Tom also has co-authored a book for the US Government published by the Washington National Press. He wrote a speech for a US Senator which was given to a joint session of Congress for which Tom received a Congressional Commendation signed by the then President.

Married for 44 years, Tom and his wife still have a very active lifestyle with a bass boat, motorcycle, and roadster sports car. And, of course, lots of traveling.

Now, at 80 years old, Tom proudly states, "My life has been and is still interesting and exciting every day."